AG
© Herbert Kruse 2001

NY
© Herbert Kruse 2001

Focke-Wulf Fw 187

In the postwar years much has been written and published about many of the aircraft developed in Germany during the Second World War. Not so the Focke Wulf Fw 187. To date, very little information has been published about this twin-engined, high-performance aircraft.
Much about this interesting aircraft remains shrouded in darkness, although the Fw 187 was a contemporary of the Messerschmitt Bf 110 and later the Me 210. This documentation is intended to shed light upon the rise and fall of the Fw 187, which was appropriately dubbed the *Falke* (Falcon).

Focke-Wulf Fw 187
An Illustrated History

Dietmar Hermann & Peter Petrick

Schiffer Military History
Atglen, PA

Translated from the German by David Johnston
Book Design by Ian Robertson.

Library of Congress Catalog Number: 2003101395

Printed in China.
ISBN: 0-7643-1871-3

This book was originally printed under the title,
Focke-Wulf Fw 187 Der vergessene Hochleistungsjäger by Aviatic Verlag

We are interested in hearing from authors with book ideas on related topics.

Published by Schiffer Publishing Ltd.
4880 Lower Valley Road
Atglen, PA 19310
Phone: (610) 593-1777
FAX: (610) 593-2002
E-mail: Schifferbk@aol.com.
Visit our web site at: www.schifferbooks.com
Please write for a free catalog.
This book may be purchased from the publisher.
Please include $3.95 postage.
Try your bookstore first.

In Europe, Schiffer books are distributed by:
Bushwood Books
6 Marksbury Avenue
Kew Gardens
Surrey TW9 4JF
England
Phone: 44 (0) 20 8392-8585
FAX: 44 (0) 20 8392-9876
E-mail: Bushwd@aol.com.
Free postage in the UK. Europe: air mail at cost.
Try your bookstore first.

Contents

Foreword

Several years ago, while researching the Focke Wulf Fw 190/ Ta 152 series of fighters, I came across a Focke Wulf development report whose contents I found baffling. The report initially concerned itself with the planned prototypes for the high-altitude fighter version of the Fw 190 equipped with an exhaust-driven turbosupercharger. Immediately following this, however, were detailed conversion plans for two old Focke Wulf Fw 187s assigned company priority level two. These Fw 187 conversions had been placed ahead of all other planned prototypes of the Fw 190 and Fw 191. The report was dated 7 August 1942. Until then, all I had known about the Fw 187 was that it was an experimental aircraft whose development had been abandoned at the start of the Second World War. Why then had the Focke Wulf Fw 187 suddenly reappeared in 1942? Had these aircraft flown? None of the existing literature offered any clues. That state of affairs provided the inspiration for this book.

It is a fact that when it first appeared, the Fw 187, which was aptly named *Falke* (Falcon), possessed a performance superior to all other German fighter aircraft. It was faster than the new Messerschmitt Bf 109, which was powered by the same type of engine. In the years before the war, the two main fighter producers, Heinkel and Messerschmitt, established a number of records with their He 100 and Me 209 aircraft. Focke Wulf was planning a record attempt with the Fw 187, however this was frustrated by the outbreak of the war.

Something that is not known, is that as a result of a requirement issued by the RLM, the two-seat Fw 187 was to have been a night-fighter and not a new *Zerstörer*, as has been generally accepted in the past. Having built the Messerschmitt Bf 110 under license, Focke Wulf would have been quite capable of switching production to the new Fw 187 night fighter, but the RLM proved short-sighted and stopped this promising development. A short time later, when night fighters became necessary, the Messerschmitt Bf 110 was converted into an interim night fighter and this makeshift solution continued until the end of the war.

Many factors came together in 1942, when the RLM again showed interest in the "old Fw 187". Suddenly the Fw 187 was to operate in the roles of night fighter, high altitude fighter and *Zerstörer*. The night fighter situation was by then plain to see, as the *Luftwaffe* had proved incapable of countering the RAF's heavy night raids. Moreover, the question of a replacement for the obsolescent Bf 110 *Zerstörer* was still open. The intended successor to the Bf 110, the Messerschmitt Me 210, had proved a failure. Aircraft like the Bf 110, which should have been replaced long before, were still flying. There, too, the Fw 187 seemed to offer a solution. The new Fw 187's greatest advantage was its use of the DB 605 engine, which was then being mass-produced for the Bf 109 fighter. Even equipped with the standard version of the DB 605, a high-altitude version of the Fw 187 would have been capable of altitudes in excess of 13 000 meters. Filled with optimism and enthusiasm, the company set to work.

During my research Dipl.Ing. Hans Sander, the most important surviving eyewitness, died. Hans Sander was Focke Wulf's chief test pilot and head of the prototype testing department. The Fw 187 was the first aircraft he flew after joining Focke Wulf. In the final days of his life he recalled flying the Fw 187.

Background

At the beginning of 1934 the *Reichsluftministerium* (RLM) issued a requirement for development of a new single-seat fighter to replace the standard fighters then in service with the *Luftwaffe*, the Heinkel He 51 and Arado Ar 68. The specification called for a fighter of all-metal construction. As well, the new fighter had to be capable of exceeding 450 km/h with a 650-h.p. engine and have a retractable undercarriage. Armament was to consist of one cannon and two rifle-caliber machine-guns. Four companies were requested to submit proposals: Arado, Focke Wulf, Heinkel and Messerschmitt. Based on the RLM specification, the four competitors developed designs which differed markedly from one another. Arado entered the Ar 80, Focke Wulf the Fw 159, Heinkel the He 112, and Messerschmitt the Bf 109. The RLM ordered prototypes of each of the types to confirm their abilities.

The histories and experiences of the competing companies naturally led to differing layouts for their designs. The design of the Messerschmitt Bf 109 was based on Messerschmitt's experience with his successful Bf 108 *Taifun* touring machine. The Bf 108 was a low-wing monoplane of all-metal construction with a retractable undercarriage. With its slotted airfoil and landing flaps, it incorporated all the features associated with a modern touring machine. The design team responsible for the Bf 109 was led by Richard Bauer, who had come to Messerschmitt from Arado. The design of the Bf 109 was clearly influenced by the Bf 108. Like the Bf 108, the Bf 109 was designed to be simple and functional. The team's objective was to design the smallest possible airframe to accommodate the most powerful engine available in Germany. Other features were leading edge slats to maintain aileron effectiveness

The Bf 109 was Messerschmitt's entry in the competition for a standard *Luftwaffe* fighter. Illustrated here is the Bf 109 V1.

The Bf 109 was an advanced design and emerged victorious from the fighter competition. (EADS, Ottobrunn Archive)

The Fw 159, a parasol monoplane, proved inferior to its monoplane competitors.

and split landing flaps. The undercarriage retracted outwards into the wing and the legs were attached to the fuselage in the wing roots. As neither the DB 600 nor the Jumo 210 was available in time for the planned first flight, the first prototype was powered by a Rolls Royce Kestrel. The Bf 109 V1 took to the air for the first time in September 1935.

A team led by Dipl.Ing. Walter Blume designed the Arado Ar 80. The Ar 80 was a cantilever gull-wing monoplane with a faired fixed undercarriage. The design was aerodynamically clean, however its performance suffered on account of its fixed undercarriage. As no suitable German engine was available for installation in the first prototype, Arado also employed a Rolls Royce Kestrel. So equipped, the Ar 80 V1 was ready for the fly-off held in Travemünde.

Focke Wulf's entry was the Fw 159. The design, developed by a team led by Dipl.Ing. Kurt Tank, was based on the successful Fw 56 *Stösser*. The Fw 56 had been designed in response to an RLM specification for an advanced fighter trainer. The parasol monoplane configuration offered an excellent view from the cockpit. Furthermore, the Fw 56 demonstrated excellent handling characteristics. All of this may have seemed good reason for Tank and his team to base the design of the Fw 159 on the proven, and the layout of the aircraft was similar to that of the Fw 56. Unlike the earlier design, however, the Fw 159 had a retractable undercarriage. The undercarriage proved to be a problem area and the V1 was damaged on its very first flight. While on approach to land, Flugkapitän Stein found that the undercarriage legs had not locked in the down position. Various maneuvers were carried out in an effort to solve the problem, but in vain. The V1 crashed on landing. Test pilot Stein was fortunate to escape with bumps and bruises.

Like the Bf 109, the Heinkel He 112 was designed as a cantilever low-wing monoplane with a retractable undercarriage. The He 112 was designed by a team under the leadership of Dr. Hertel. The all-metal monoplane was an aerodynamically clean design with an elliptical wing characteristic of Heinkel designs. The first prototype was the He 112 V1, D-IADO. It, too, was powered by a Rolls Royce Kestrel engine producing 695 h.p. In terms of performance,

The Heinkel He 112 provided the Bf 109 with its most serious competition. Illustrated here is the He 112 V1.

the He 112 was the only aircraft which could compete with the Bf 109.

The first comparison flights between the four competitors took place in Travemünde at the end of October 1935. Realistically, the Arado Ar 80 and the Fw 159 had no chance against the more modern Bf 109 and He 112. Neither of the two last-named machines was short on speed, both achieving maximum speeds of 470 km/h at an altitude of 3 300 meters. With an initial climb rate of 13.7 m/sec, the Bf 109 was slightly superior to the He 112. The close results in the fly-off resulted in pre-production contracts from the RLM for both the He 112 and Bf 109. While Heinkel was actually slightly ahead with its He 112, other criteria decided the race for the standard fighter in favor of the Bf 109. While Messerschmitt retained the design layout of the first Bf 109 for production aircraft, the Heinkel underwent numerous changes. Furthermore, the Bf 109 was simpler to build and was therefore cheaper and quicker to mass-produce. It also proved to be capable of a superior performance. The He 112 was redesigned in an attempt to win the contest for Heinkel, however these constant design changes had exactly the opposite result. Messerschmitt's Bf 109 won the competition.

After the Bf 109 was selected to be the *Luftwaffe*'s standard day fighter, Focke Wulf abandoned work on the Fw 159. The parasol monoplane configuration was surpassed by its low-wing monoplane competitors and from the beginning it had practically no chance. Indeed, the design became the subject of jokes. In RLM circles the Fw 159 was given the derogatory nickname *Trampel* (clod or klutz), because of its complicated undercarriage retraction mechanism. The Fw 259, a development of the Fw 159 powered by a DB 600 engine, was also dropped. The Fw 159 project was a flop. The sneering comments worsened the situation for Prof. Tank and his team. The company and Prof. Kurt Tank, in particular, drew their conclusions. From this painful setback Dipl.Ing. Tank conceived the idea of a twin-engined, single seat high-performance fighter aircraft.

The Custom-Made Design

In the beginning, there was no direct official development contract for the Fw 187. The company, and Kurt Tank in particular, hoped that a developed project might awaken the interest of the RLM and secure for the company a desperately-needed contract. Leading the Fw 187 project was Professor Kurt Tank, who placed *Oberingenieur* Rudolf Blaser in charge of the design work. The principal objective of the Fw 187's designers was to reduce drag and thus achieve a high maximum speed. In keeping with the objective of minimizing drag, the fuselage cross-section was kept very narrow. At its widest point it was no wider than that of a conventional single-engine fighter aircraft. Every aspect of the Fw 187 was designed to keep drag to a minimum.

Focke Wulf subsequently tried to interest the RLM in the idea of a high-performance twin-engined fighter aircraft. The entire project was shown to the Technical Office's development section, which was then under the direction of *Oberst* W. von Richthofen. From the outset the Focke Wulf project appeared extremely promising and was therefore assessed positively. Department LC II of the RLM was subsequently instructed to issue a development contract corresponding to the specifications provided by Focke Wulf. The contract was issued to the company in November 1935. Focke Wulf had finally received the official contract for the project it had been seeking. Von Richthofen promised that there would be no interference from the Technical Office and that Tank was to decide on all technical questions. Focke Wulf was instructed to build three prototypes. The fighter was officially designated the Fw 187 *Falke*.

From the very beginning the Fw 187 was conceived as a cantilever low-wing monoplane of all-metal stressed-skin construction. The wing center-section also formed the fuselage center-section and, together with the engine nacelles, formed a single unit. It was initially anticipated that the aircraft would be powered by two Daimler Benz DB 600 engines each producing 960 h.p., however these were not available. Focke Wulf opted for the Junkers Jumo 210, a less powerful engine. At that time the Jumo 210 had a maximum output of 610 h.p. at an altitude of 4 000 meters. As early as 28 March 1936 Focke Wulf identified that so-called hot-cooling

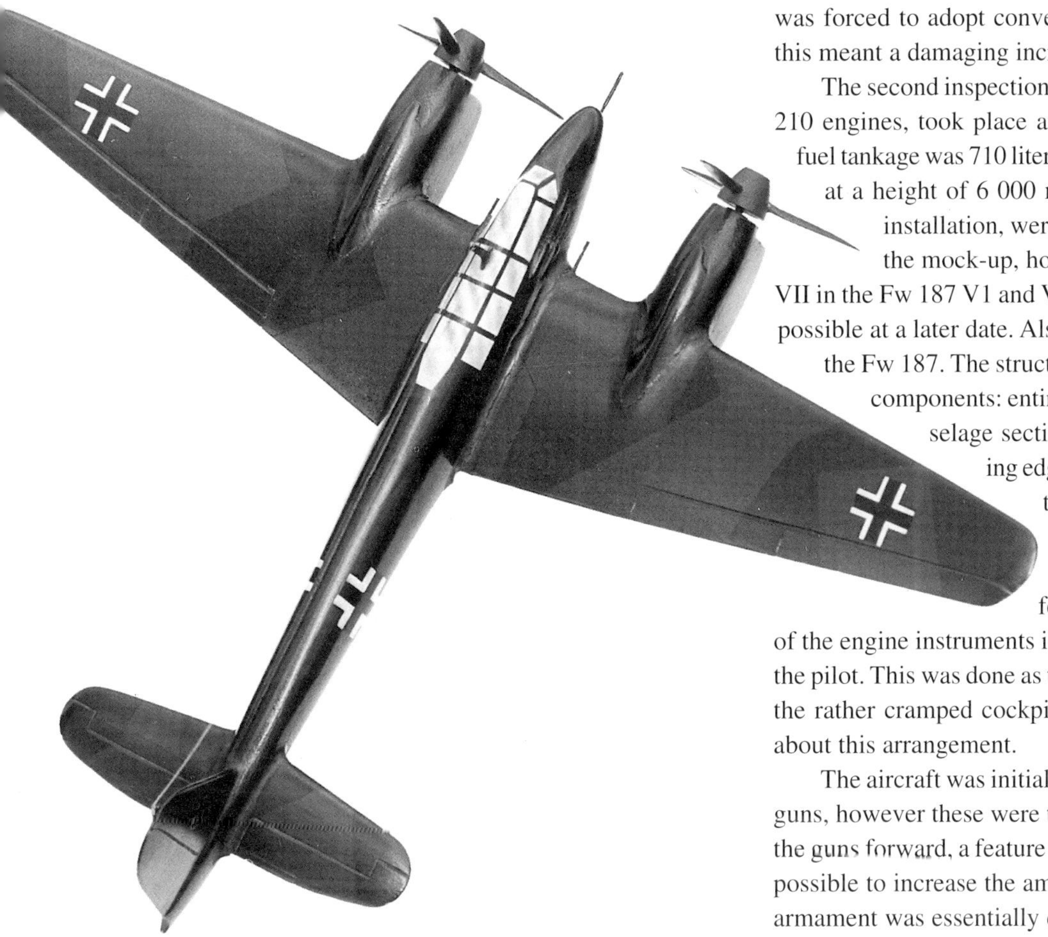

for the Jumo 210 engines was necessary to achieve a successful Fw 187. The advantage of hot-cooled engines lay in the reduction of the amount of cooling necessary for the engines. This meant smaller radiators and thus reduced drag. At that time hot-cooling tests with the Jumo 210 were running into problems, however, and Focke Wulf was forced to adopt conventional water cooling. For the Fw 187 this meant a damaging increase in drag.

The second inspection of the Fw 187 mock-up, now with Jumo 210 engines, took place at the beginning of 1936. Total planned fuel tankage was 710 liters. Endurance was two hours at full power at a height of 6 000 meters. Other details, such as the radio installation, were finalized. The FuG VI was installed in the mock-up, however it was planned to install the FuG VII in the Fw 187 V1 and V2. Installation of the FuG XII was to be possible at a later date. Also finalized was the breakdown plan for the Fw 187. The structure was to be divided into the following components: entire tail section with fuselage tail cone, fuselage section between empennage and wing trailing edge, wing center section with fuselage center section, power plants, outer wings, and forward fuselage.

One of the most interesting design features of the Fw 187 was the placement of the engine instruments in the sides of the engine nacelles facing the pilot. This was done as there was no room for the instruments in the rather cramped cockpit. The RLM expressed no reservations about this arrangement.

The aircraft was initially armed with just two MG 17 machine-guns, however these were to be augmented at a later date. Moving the guns forward, a feature included in the mock-up, would make it possible to increase the ammunition load. From the beginning the armament was essentially dependent on that of the Messerschmitt Bf 109. The Fw 187's main undercarriage consisted of forked main legs which were retracted hydraulically. Mainwheel doors covered the undercarriage bays and ensured an aerodynamically clean surface. The tailwheel was also fully retractable. The radiators were located directly beneath the Jumo 210 engines, which drove VDM variable-pitch propellers.

The First Fw 187 Takes to the Air

In January 1936, just two months after the issuing of the contract by the RLM, Focke Wulf was able to display the Fw 187 mock-up. On 1 April 1936 Focke Wulf issued a detailed Specification of the Fw 187. Unfortunately it appears that this Specification has not survived to the present day. Nevertheless, some pertinent data about the single-seat machine is known. Planned performance included an endurance of two hours at an altitude of 6 000 meters at full power. Required fuel capacity was 700 liters.

In May 1936 a meeting was held between the RLM, Junkers and Focke Wulf. The Jumo 210 D was specified as the power plant for the V1, while the later Fw 187 V2 and V3 were to have the Jumo 210 G. The maiden flight of the Fw 187 V1 was planned for December 1936, however this was later postponed until the spring of 1937.

Fw 187 V1 cockpit assembly. Note the cut-out for the port fuselage machine-gun. (Petrick)

Final assembly of the Fw 187 V1 in the Bremen factory. In the foreground is the rear fuselage with stabilizer, while the engine nacelles may be seen in the background. (EADS Unternehmensarchiv Bremen)

Side and rear views of the Fw 187 V1. (Sengfelder)

On 10 April 1937 all was ready and the Fw 187 V1 waited for its first takeoff. The prototype was readied for flight on the company airfield in Bremen. Things became serious. Would the Fw 187 be able to achieve the expected performance? Would the Fw 187 make up for the company's two previous failures, the Fw 57 and Fw 159?

At precisely 16:44 hours Kurt Tank took the Fw 187 V1, serial number 949, into the air for the first time. The aircraft was as yet unpainted and did not yet bear its manufacturer's code, D-AXAK. The flight proceeded without serious problems and confirmed the quality of the development work that had preceded it. Subsequent testing was placed in the hands of company test pilot Dipl.Ing. Hans Sander. His first flights in the Fw 187 V1 revealed that it was almost impossible to maintain an absolutely correct indicated airspeed. He therefore had installed a slightly elevated pitot tube projecting in front of the aircraft nose. Subsequently dubbed the "Trombone", the new pitot made it possible to take precise readings from an area of undisturbed airflow. The Trombone was a feature of all subsequent Fw 187s.

Reflecting the advanced state of aerodynamic design in 1937, the Fw 187 had clean flowing lines with few drag-producing excrescences. Here test pilot Hans Sander is seen standing in front of the Fw 187.

Rear fuselage of the Fw 187 V1. The fin and rudder have yet to be installed.

Test Pilot Hans Sanders Assesses the Fw 187

On 1 April 1937 Focke Wulf hired a new test pilot for its expanding test flying program, *Flugbaumeister* Dipl.Ing. Hans Sander. His task was to conduct initial flights in prototypes and conduct subsequent trials up to the conclusion of type testing. He was also required to carry out demonstration and test flights for the contractors. Hans Sander's first job on joining Focke Wulf was to take over the Fw 187 test program. He summed up his impressions of the Fw 187 V1 as follows:

The Fw 187 V1 was the first prototype I flew after joining Focke Wulf as a test pilot. It was a very fast aircraft, faster than the Bf 110 and the He 112 with the Jumo 210 D. My initial flights in the Fw 187 V1 revealed a speed of 525 km/h at low level, which was 225 km/h faster than the *Luftwaffe*'s standard day fighters at that time (He 51 and Ar 68). It was approximately 35 to 40 km/h faster than the Bf 109 with the same engine at the same altitude. Furthermore it had a significantly greater range and payload. I could have set a number of world records with the machine, however those in charge did not wish that. With its four MG 17 machine-guns, later supplemented by two MG FF cannon, this was the aircraft that our air force lacked later in the war. The pilot had an excellent view for takeoff, in flight and for landing, including downwards, as there was a large clear panel in the floor. The controls were well harmonized, although their effectiveness and immediate reaction did not achieve the perfection of the later Fw 190. This was because the system of aerodynamic balancing with Flettner tabs resulted in a certain amount of play and softness. As development work was soon ended by order of the RLM, there was no opportunity to address this shortcoming. Later, when the aircraft was used by a Focke Wulf Industry Defense Flight (*Industrieschutz-Schwarm*), ballast was installed, making it possible to achieve a smooth three-point landing. The aircraft could be flown hands off on one engine. It could be easily turned into the running engine, and, with the necessary caution, also into the dead engine. A special lateral trim simplified single-engined flight and compensated for yaw and the necessary dangling over the running engine. In the beginning, aerobatics in a twin-engined machine was something

Dipl.Ing. Hans Sander played a major role in the flight testing of the Fw 187. Like many test pilots, he came from Rechlin. Sander, who went on to become chief test pilot and head of prototype testing, remained with Focke Wulf until the end of the war.

Ready to go. The Fw 187 V1 photographed in front of the hangar doors at Bremen.

Excellent flying shot of the Fw 187 V1. When this photograph was taken the aircraft still had not received its registration or camouflage paint.

new to me. I had come from Rechlin, where I was responsible for the testing of bomber aircraft and consequently had few opportunities for aerobatics. The amount of inertia produced by the two engines made aerobatics in the Fw 187 something quite different than in a single-engine machine, for example the later Fw 190. With its great range and payload, the Fw 187 was actually the prototype for our modern fighter aircraft. It is a well-known fact that most modern single-seat jet fighters have twin engines."

The testing program also required Hans Sander to conduct steep dives in order to determine the limiting speed of the Fw 187. Although the calculated limiting speed was 1 000 km/h, *Oberingenieur* Blaser predicted that flutter would begin between 750 and 830 km/h. This flutter was extremely dangerous because it would make the aircraft uncontrollable and might ultimately result in a crash. An additional counterweight was installed to prevent flutter from developing. Blaser assured Sander that the weight would prevent flutter provided he did not exceed 740 km/h in the dive. Sander took off on a test flight and after reaching the required altitude put the aircraft into a power dive. The aircraft accelerated rapidly. At 735 km/h the tail surfaces began to vibrate and Sander was no longer able to control the aircraft. He was about to abandon the V1 when he felt a hefty jolt. The vibration ceased abruptly and the V1 once again reacted to the controls. After a successful landing the V1 was immediately inspected. It was soon discovered that the additional coun-

Meeting of generations. In the background on the Focke Wulf company airfield a Fw 58 *Weihe* and Fw 44 biplane, while in the foreground the modern Fw 187 starts its engines. (Sengfelder)

terweight had cased the problem. As soon as the vibration caused it to fall away, the control surface was again in balance and the Fw 187 handled completely normally. This was probably one of the memorable moments of Hans Sander's flying career. Things could have ended much differently.

The Fw 187 V1 displayed no serious design flaws during the course of testing. It was found, however, that coolant temperatures in the climb with high-altitude superchargers on were less than 1 (approximately 0.9). Consequently tests with the Jumo engine system could only be conducted in the climb with the low-altitude superchargers on. Beginning with the Fw 187 V2, this problem was eliminated by a revised radiator fairing arrangement.

Completion of the Fw 187 V2 and V3

In the late spring of 1937, while the Fw 187 V2 was in the final stages of construction, the aircraft underwent an equipment inspection. At that time the V2 was 85% complete. Among those who took part in the inspection were Focke Wulf staff, representatives of the *E-Stelle Rechlin* and quality control officials. In order to hasten testing of the V2 by the *E-Stelle Rechlin*, the planned radio equipment was dispensed with. The only complaints by the quality control officials concerned minor details of the aircraft's electrical system. For example, they wanted the pitot heat system connected to the aircraft's electrical system on a separate circuit with its own circuit breaker.

Although it had been planned otherwise, the second prototype was fitted with Jumo 210 D carburetor engines and VDM variable-pitch propellers exactly like those of the V1. The V2 (serial number 950) did incorporate a number of changes, however, mainly in the area of the control surfaces. The radiator fairings were also modified. The V2 took to the air on its maiden flight in June 1937. It is not known for certain if Kurt Tank was the pilot. An entry concerning a maintenance test flight suggests that he did, as the V1 was already wearing the registration D-AXAK. Tank carried out a number of test flights in the Fw 187 V2 at Bremen on 30 September and 28 October 1937. Although Focke Wulf had initially planned to conduct tests with the V2 to accurately measure radiator performance, as desired by the test station, orders arrived for the prototype to be sent to Rechlin as soon as the factory received the variable-pitch propellers. The Fw 187 V2 was thus flown to Rechlin soon after it was completed with only brief factory trials. In Rechlin the V2 was tested extensively as part of the type certification program.

Though of poor quality, this is the only known photograph of the Fw 187 V2 which provides a complete side view.

The Fw 187 V2 parked in front of the Focke Wulf hangar doors. (Focke Wulf)

The Fw 187 V2 with experimental twin-wheel main undercarriage. (Herwig)

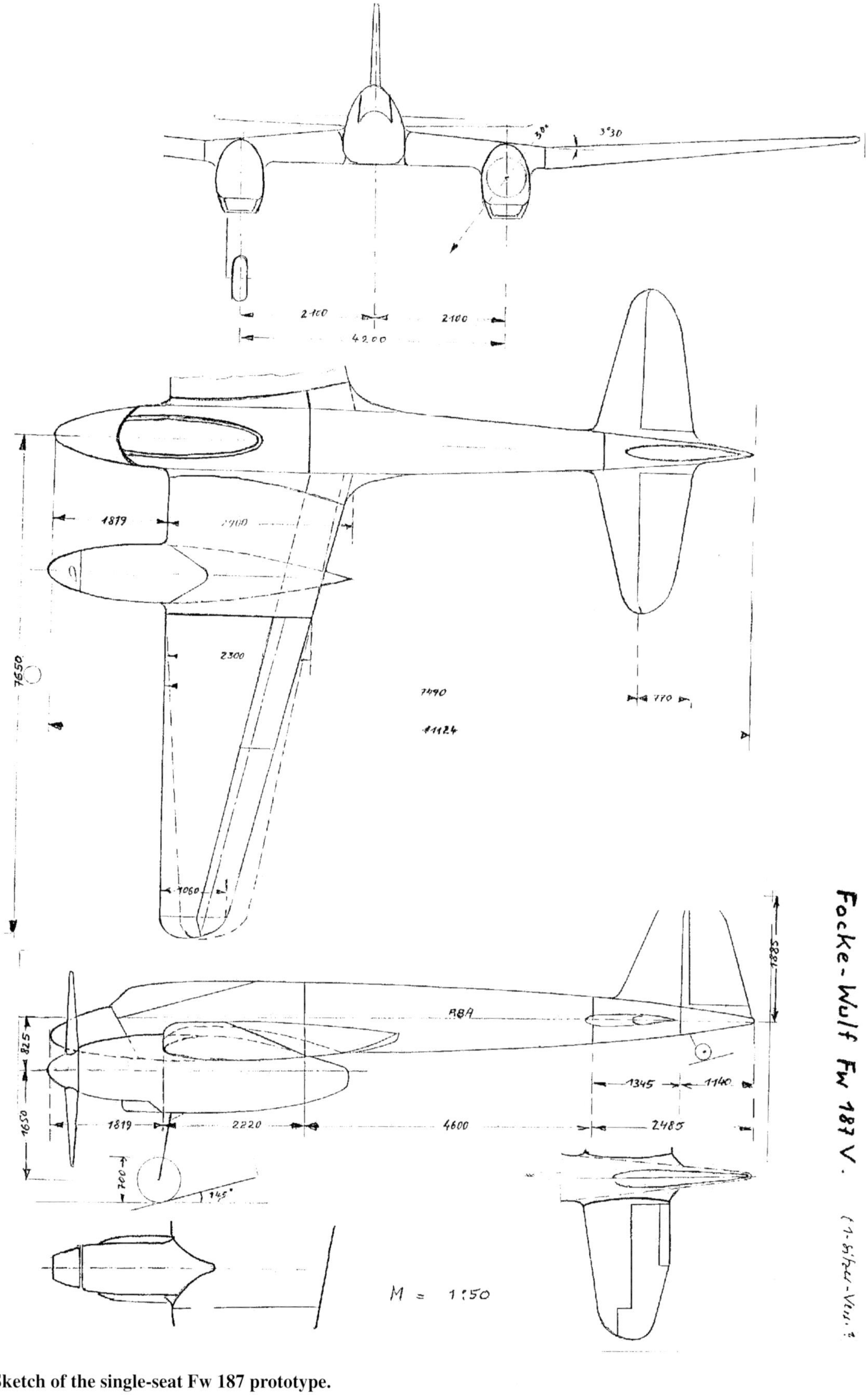

Sketch of the single-seat Fw 187 prototype.

Engine start-up by the Fw 187 V2. A Focke Wulf technician cleans the windscreen in preparation for a test flight. (Herwig)

In the course of testing at Rechlin the following performance figures were recorded: with a takeoff weight of 3 850 kg the fighter achieved a maximum speed of 457 km/h at low level and 501 km/h at an altitude of 3 000 meters (2,7000 rpm, boost pressure 1.26 atm). Service ceiling was 9 250 meters (0.5 m/sec rate of climb), at which height the V2's speed was 336 km/h. The aircraft was found to have an outstanding rate of climb, 17.5 m/sec at low level. There was little decrease in the aircraft's rate of climb as altitude increased. At 2 000 meters it was still 16 m/sec. This was reflected in times to climb. The V2 proved capable of reaching 4 000 meters in 4.5 minutes, while just eight minutes were required to reach 6 000 meters. The aircraft's single-engine flight characteristics were also extensively investigated in Rechlin. The Rechlin test pilots found that the Fw 187 could climb on one engine and that the aircraft was capable of going around on a single engine. It is interesting that exhaust gas measurements were carried out at that time. Measurements were taken in the climb, dive and level flight as well as in a left turn. In each case the values measured were below the limiting value of 0.0025%.

At the very least. Plans were made for the equipment of the Fw 187 V2 with more powerful Jumo 210 G motors. In March 1938 the V2 was back in Rechlin, as test pilot Pfister carried out flights in the aircraft on the 19th. On 22 March 1938 the V2 suffered an undercarriage failure resulting from a faulty weld. Damage was minor and the aircraft was repaired within a week. The famous test pilot Heinrich Beauvais made the last known flights at Rechlin by the V2, on 3 and 10 October 1938. After these final flights the trail of the Fw 187 V2 vanishes. Nothing is known of its fate following delivery to the RLM on 2 August 1939.

Relatively little is known about the Fw 187 V3, serial number 1707. It was the third and last prototype of the Fw 187 experimental single-seat fighter. It was to have incorporated all the improvements which flowed from testing of the first two prototypes. From the beginning, the V3 was equipped with more powerful Jumo 210 G fuel-injected engines. These engines were also equipped with ejector-style exhausts. For improved cooling, the V3's radiators were approximately 15% larger than those of the V2. The V3 was also intended to be the Fw 187 armament test bed. At the request of the *Chef LC* the aircraft was fitted with armament and subsequently tested at Rechlin beginning in late September 1938. Initial air firing trials began on 29 September. From then on the Fw 187 V3 visited Rechlin often. Its last known flight there was on 24 November 1939 in the hands of Heinrich Beauvais. As the photographs reveal, the V3 was involved in a landing accident. To date no details of the incident are known.

Prior to the accident, Kurt Tank flew the machine from Bremen on several occasions at the beginning of September 1938. Tank's first flight in the aircraft, registered D-AODE, took place on 4 September 1938. The aircraft's maiden flight must also have taken place at about that time. On 24 September in Bremen Tank gave a demonstration in the V3 which lasted 48 minutes, an unusually long time for such a flight. No matter how impressive, this demonstration could not alter the fate of the single-seat version.

The following reproduction of the Fw 187 V2 type test report reveals the aircraft's excellent performance. It is the sole surviving performance report on the single-seat Fw 187. The Fw 187 V2 had an outstanding low-level climb rate, 17.5 m/sec. This was fully com-

Two interesting photographs of Fw 187s on jacks. At the top is the Fw 187 V1 with the standard undercarriage and below the Fw 187 V2 with the experimental twin-wheel undercarriage. (Sengfelder, Herwig)

Rechlin E 7c p Erpr.Nr. 1402 Teilbericht 10	Flugzeug Fw 187 V 2 Musterprüfung und Flugleistungen.	Musterprüfbericht 152 f. PfL-Auftr. vom 16.8.37 Blatt 2

Inhalt!

1.) Allgemeines:

Flugzeug: Fw 187 V 2
Werk-Nr. 950

Motoren: 2 x Jumo 210 D
Werk-Nr. 40155
Werk-Nr. 40610

Luftschrauben: 2 x HKW Verstellschraube 3 flg.
Werk-Nr. 17310
Werk-Nr. 17311 D = 3000 mm
12^{00} Uhr = 25° Blattwinkel

Fluggewicht: G = 3850 kg

2.) Abflugleistung:

Start Nr.	Anlauf m	Anlauf sec	Von Stand bis 20 m Höhe m	Von Stand bis 20 m Höhe sec	Abehebegeschw. km/h	Luftschrauben=stellung
1	164	10,50	421	17,70	117	12.00
2	142	9,7	386	16,80	103	12.00
3	154	10,2	402	17,20	111	12.00

Extract from a Rechlin test report on the Focke Wulf Fw 187 V2.

Rechlin E 7c$_p$ Erpr.Nr. 1402 Teilbericht 10	Flugzeug Fw 187 V 2 Musterprüfung und Flugleistungen.	Musterprüfbericht 152 f. PfL-Auftr. vom 16.8.37 Blatt 3

3.) Landeleistung:

Landung Nr.	Auslauf m	Auslauf sec	Von 20 m Höhe bis Stillstand m	Von 20 m Höhe bis Stillstand sec	Landegeschw. km/h	Luftschrauben=stellung
1	448	19,6	726	26,8	139	12.00
2	439	22,5	817	32,4	129	12.00
3	486	21,4	797	29,6	135	12.00

Sämtliche Werte von 2) und 3) sind auf Normaltag umgerechnet (0 m/sec Wind; γ_0 = 1,225 kg/m^3).

4.) Steigleistung:

Höhe (INA) km	Steiggeschw. m/sec	Steigzeit min	Bahngeschw. V_w km/h	Drehzahlen min^{-1}	Lade=druck ata	Bemerkun=gen
0	17,5	--	246	2700	1,28	
1	15,9	1,0	258	2700	1,28	
2	16,0	2,1	268	2700	1,28	
3	14,4	3,2	276	2700	1,19	
4	12,2	4,5	280	2700	1,06	
5	10,0	6,2	280	2700	0,93	
6	7,8	8,0	280	2700	0,80	
7	5,5	10,3	280	2700	0,67	
8	3,3	14,3	284	2700	0,54	
9	1,1	22,5	295	2700	0,41	
9,25	0,5	27,5	300	2700	0,38	Dienst=gipfelh.

Extract from a Rechlin test report on the Focke Wulf Fw 187 V2.

The Fw 187 V2 at Rechlin following an undercarriage failure. As the following photographs show, the undercarriage was the Achilles heel of the early prototypes. Note the muzzle of the starboard MG 17. (Herwig)

Rechlin E 7c$_p$ Erpr.Nr. 1402 Teilbericht 10	Flugzeug Fw 187 V 2 Musterprüfung und Flugleistungen.	Musterprüfbericht 152 f. PfL-Auftr. vom 16.8.37 Blatt 4

5.) Geschwindigkeitsleistung:

Höhe (INA) km	Höchstgeschw. V_w km/h	Drehzahlen min^{-1}	Ladedruck ata	Bemerkungen
0	457	2700	1,28	
1	466	2700	1,28	
2	463	2700	1,28	
3	501	2700	1,26	
4	496	2700	1,14	
5	489	2700	1,01	
6	478	2700	0,89	
7	461	2700	0,77	
8	430	2700	0,63	
9	362	2700	0,45	
9,25	336	2700	0,40	Dienstgipfelhöhe

6.) Einmotorenleistung:

Der Einmotorenflug wurde mit dem BB-Motor in 1500 m Höhe durchgeführt. Der St.B.-Motor lief im Leerlauf mit. Es ist möglich, mit einem Motor noch zu steigen. Durchstarten einmotorig möglich.

7.) CO-Messung:

Die CO-Messungen in der Fw 187/950 ergaben:

Steigflug : 0,0008 % CO
Gleitflug : 0,0011 % CO
Reiseflug : 0,0002 % CO
Linkskurve : 0,0004 % CO

In allen gemessenen Flugzuständen liegen die Werte unter der zulässigen Grenze von 0,0025 % CO.

Extract from a Rechlin test report on the Focke Wulf Fw 187 V2 listing speeds at various altitudes. During trials at Rechlin the V2 achieved 457 km/h at low level and 501 km/h at the maximum boost altitude of 3000 m. The report states that the Fw 187 was capable of climbing on one engine and could also carry out a go-around.

Two close-ups of the collapsed undercarriage of D-AANA. Note the engine instruments in the engine nacelle just forward of the leading edge. (Herwig)

Two photographs of D-AODE after a crash-landing. The V3 introduced several significant improvements. In contrast to the V1 and V2, the aircraft was powered by more powerful Jumo 210 G engines with ejector exhausts and capped spinners. The curved windscreen was also replaced by a new design incorporating flat panels.

parable to the climb rate of the later Fw 190 single-engine fighter, one of the most successful fighters in the world.

The V3 began testing somewhat later than the other prototypes. In April 1937 Focke Wulf was anticipating that the V3 would fly in April, however the RLM demanded a number of changes to improve flight safety. These included separate circuits for the identification lights, instrument panel lighting, pitot tube heat and electric turn and bank indicator, and mechanical undercarriage position indicators. As well, Focke Wulf used a large number of specialized devices for the undercarriage position monitoring system, approval of which would depend on the results of testing by the *E-Stelle Rechlin*. As a result of these changes, the date for the aircraft to be ready to fly was put back to November 1937. Were these demands an indication of the RLM's waning interest in the single-seat Fw 187?

View from the pilot's seat of the Fw 187. Note the fully packed instrument panel. As this photograph clearly shows, the pilot of the Fw 187 had an excellent all-round view. The window in the floor even provided the pilot with a downward view. This blown-hood design placed Focke Wulf ahead of its contemporaries. Inexplicably, this type of canopy was not adopted for Focke Wulf's next twin-engined design, the Ta 154, which had a much poorer view from the cockpit. (Focke Wulf)

Close-ups of the left and right consoles of the Fw 187 V2. The floor window extended back to the pilot's seat. The bulged channels just below the cockpit sill on both sides were intended to accommodate the barrels of the planned MG 17 machine-guns.

The Westland Whirlwind Great Britain's Fw 187

In the United Kingdom, aircraft designers were working on a single-seat twin-engined fighter even as Focke Wulf was developing the early Fw 187. Westland Aircraft Ltd. developed and built the Whirlwind fighter in response to Air Ministry specification F.37/35. Two prototypes were ordered, and the first, L 6844, took to the air on 11 October 1938, a good year and a half after the maiden flight of the Fw 187. Unlike the single-seat version of the Fw 187, however, the Westland Whirlwind entered front-line service in 1940. An initial order was placed for 400 Whirlwinds. No. 263 Squadron began operating the type from Exeter on 7 December 1940. The type achieved considerable success, first as a long-range escort fighter and later as a high-speed fighter-bomber. The Achilles' Heel of the Whirlwind was its trouble-prone Rolls Royce Peregrine engines. High-altitude performance was poor, and spare parts were hard to come by. For all these reasons, production of the Whirlwind was halted after the 112th machine.

The Westland Whirlwind came as an unpleasant surprise to the German air force. While the Bf 110 had proved inferior to the Spitfire in a dogfight, the maneuverability and speed of the Whirlwind made it a match even for the Messerschmitt Bf 109, and a number of the German fighters were claimed shot down by Whirlwind pilots. With its range and endurance, more than twice that of the Bf 109, the Whirlwind was also capable of mounting fighter-bomber raids against German airfields in France. On 18 August 1941 Whirlwinds escorted Bristol Blenheims in a daylight raid on Cologne, confirming the philosophy put forward by Kurt Tank.

It was claimed that a Whirlwind equipped with more powerful Rolls Royce Merlin engines could have achieved speeds on the order of 680 km/h, however the necessary modifications to accommodate the more powerful Merlins were never carried out. Problems with its Peregrine power plants denied the Whirlwind even greater success. By 1943 the Whirlwinds had been replaced by the new Mosquito.

Powered by two 885-h.p. engines, the Westland Whirlwind achieved 576 km/h at a height of 4570 meters. Unlike the Fw 187, it entered production. Though the Whirlwind was built in small numbers, it demonstrated the correctness of the twin-engined fighter philosophy.

Performance Comparison: Westland Whirlwind and the Fw 187

The following table provides a detailed comparison of the performances of the two contemporaries. As a result of the inferior performance of the Jumo 210 D engines, the Fw 187's maximum speed was lower than that of the Whirlwind. The Fw 187 V3 was equipped with the Jumo 210 G, which produced 730 h.p. and was fitted with ejector-type exhausts producing a certain amount of thrust. No test results for the V3 have survived nor are there any detailed performance estimates. It is to be assumed, however, that the V3's maximum speed would have been much closer to that of the Whirlwind. The wing loading of the Fw 187 was much less than is often claimed. Although the Fw 187 was somewhat larger than the Whirlwind, it was almost one ton lighter.

It was originally planned that the Fw 187 would be armed with two 7.92-mm machine-guns, however later plans called for a more powerful armament of two 20-mm MG FF cannon and two 7.92-mm machine-guns. The Whirlwind, on the other hand, was powerfully armed from the beginning, with four 20-mm cannon mounted centrally in the fuselage nose in an arrangement similar to that of the later Me 262 jet fighter. The Whirlwind was also capable of carrying 454 kilograms of bombs. There were no plans to employ the Fw 187 in the fighter-bomber role.

Designation	**Focke Wulf Fw 187 V1**	**Westland Whirlwind Mk 1**
Purpose	Single-seat, twin-engined fighter	Single-seat, twin-engined fighter
Empty weight	ca. 2500 kg	3770 kg
Gross weight	3850 kg	4700 kg
Wingspan	15.30 m	13.72 m
Length	11.124 m	9.98 m
Height	3.35 m	3.5 2 m
Wing area	30.00 m2	23.22 rn 2
Wing loading	128.33 kg/m2	222.48 kg /m2
Power plants	2 xJumo 210 D	2 x RR Peregrine 1
Takeoff power	2 x 680 PS	2 x 885 PS
Fuel	B 4/87 Octane	87 Octane
Fuel capacity	7101	6101
Range	1000 km	1290 km
Landing speed	139 km/h	157 km/h
Speed at low level	457	506 km/h in 1.5 km Höhe
Maximum speed at	501 km/h	576 km/h
maximum boost altitude	3 km	4.57 km
Rate of climb at low level	17.5 m/s	ca. 15 m/s
Times to climb	3.2 min. to 3000 m	4.0 min. to 3050 m
	4.5 min. to 4000 m	5.8 min. to 4570 m
	8.0 min. to 6000 m	8.6 min. to 6060 m
Service ceiling	9.25 km	9.1 km
Fuselage armament	2 x 7.92 mm MG 17	4 x 20 mm MK Hispano Mk. 1
Bomb load	keine	max. 454 kg

A duel that never took place: the Westland Whirlwind versus the Focke Wulf Fw 187 Falke.

The Crash of Fw 187 V1

At the end of 1937 a new test pilot, Paul Bauer, joined Focke Wulf. According to Hans Sander, Bauer was a daring test pilot and parachutist. Bauer took little time in adjusting to his new surroundings and was soon assisting Hans Sander in testing the Fw 187. He flew the Fw 187 extremely well and knew how to get the best out of the machine, especially in aerobatics. What he lacked, however, was a thorough background in technical training. His willingness to take risks was to cost him dearly.

On 15 May 1938 Focke Wulf test pilot Paul Bauer was killed in the crash of the Fw 187 V1 during a test flight.

This is probably the first in-flight photograph of the Fw 187 V1 ever published. No markings have yet been applied.

Viewed from behind, the clean lines of the Fw 187 are obvious. In this photograph the engines of the V1 are being serviced.

Preparations before a flight by the Fw 187 V1. The pilot is most likely Paul Bauer. (Sengfelder)

On 14 May 1938, during aerobatics training in the Fw 187 V1, Paul Bauer was killed when the aircraft crashed. After a steep dive to ground level, he pulled the Fw 187 V1 up into a loop. The aircraft lost too much speed and entered a spin. Out of control, the V1 crashed to the earth. In this extreme situation Bauer attempted to bale out. He succeeded in jettisoning the canopy and releasing his straps, however he failed to get out of the aircraft before it struck the ground. He was buried in Hamburg. The company held a minute of silence in his honor. The RLM is alleged to have used the crash as an excuse not to order a procurement program for the Fw 187. This claim is repeated in numerous publications. This is too simple an explanation, however. Many later successful aircraft suffered crashes. Even aircraft whose success appeared questionable from the beginning entered production. One only has to recall the He 177, which went through a series of crashes resulting in the type being nicknamed the "Reich Cigarette Lighter". Moreover, the crash of the Fw 187 was due to pilot error, not a design flaw.

Other arguments for the cancellation of the single-seat Fw 187 are more convincing. Göring was firmly convinced that two engines were too many for a fighter aircraft and his views carried weight in the RLM. As Hans Sander put it, at that time the *Luftwaffe* did not yet realize the need for a twin-engined escort fighter with long range. Not until near the end of the war was the correctness of this philosophy acknowledged, resulting in the rushed development of the Do 335, which never proceeded past the test phase.

In any case, by May 1938 the fate of the single-seat fighter version was sealed. Preliminary discussions concerning a twin-seat version of the Fw 187 had taken place some time earlier. Indeed a mock-up of the two-seat version was inspected by the RLM in December 1937.

The Fw 187 from Rechlin's Point of View

Rechlin Test Pilot Heinrich Beauvais: "Like the Focke Wulf Fw 58 and the Messerschmitt Bf 110, the Fw 187 started out as a C2 aircraft. As a result, I was not required to fly it at first. Before long, however, I was called upon to make a maintenance test flight, because the pilot in charge of flight operations did not trust this strange single-seater with no flight engineer. The type also had a high wing loading, roughly equivalent to that of a Ju 52, and required rather quicker reactions than the other single-seaters, but otherwise it was not difficult to handle. It was faster than the 109 and had a greater range. Why I do not recall any comparison flights with the 109 and 110 I cannot say. I was less impressed by its poor maneuverability while taxiing. I recall having observed some elevator flutter which was said to have been caused by separation of the Flettner tab's counterweights."

D-AANA visited Rechlin on numerous occasions.

Second Chance as a *Zerstörer*?

On 20 January 1937 an important conference was held in the RLM concerning future aircraft development programs for the *Luftwaffe*. There it was decided that work on the three Fw 187 prototypes would continue as before, but that work on the eleven preproduction aircraft was to cease. This decision was confirmed by the head of the department soon afterwards, on 12 February 1937. The RLM had thus rejected Kurt Tank's idea of a fast long-range escort fighter. The single-seat Fw 187 was not going to be produced as a twin-engined air-superiority fighter.

The RLM clung to the *Zerstörer*, or strategic fighter, concept for the new *Luftwaffe*. The multipurpose *Kampfzerstörer* demanded by the RLM's Technical Office was to be capable of the following roles:

1. Penetrate deep into enemy airspace to clear the sky of enemy fighters ahead of the bomber formations.
2. Escort bomber formations.
3. Intercept and destroy enemy bombers a long distance from their targets.
4. Fighter-bomber attacks deep in the enemy rear.

The heavy Fw 57 was not adopted for the *Zerstörer* role. (Focke Wulf)

The issuing of contracts for the *Kampfzerstörer* did not come as the result of a direct competition as in the case of the standard fighter specification. The RLM initially conceived a twin-engined design with a heavy defensive armament. The *Kampfzerstörer* was to be capable of operating as a bomber, bomber escort or bomber interceptor, but it also had to be able to operate in the reconnaissance and close-support roles. Several well-known aircraft companies submitted designs. AGO's Ao 225 and Gotha's 3001 and 3002, the latter twin-fuselage designs, proceeded no farther than the drawing board, while the most promising designs—the Focke Wulf Fw 57, the Henschel Hs 124, and the Messerschmitt Bf 110—were proceeded with. It initially appeared that the decision would fall on one of two designs, Focke Wulf's Fw 57 or Henschel's Hs 124.

The Fw 57 was the creation of a design team headed by Dipl.Ing. Bansemir and was conceived as a cantilever low-wing monoplane with twin engines and a retractable undercarriage. The fuselage was an all-metal monocoque structure of oval cross-section. The three-piece wing was also an all-metal structure with three spars. The main undercarriage retracted rearwards into the engine nacelles. The Fw 57 was designed for a crew of three: pilot, radio operator and gunner. One of the most interesting features of the Fw 57 was its unusual electrically-powered dorsal turret. The idea of equipping a fighter with a powered turret was not unique to Germany, however. Great Britain produced the Boulton Paul Defiant and Blackburn Roc, both single-engined machines with powered turrets. The Fw 57 was initially designed to take two Jumo 210 G engines, with which it was hopelessly underpowered. Only the more powerful Daimler Benz DB 600 producing 910 h.p. could have made the Fw 57 competitive. The Fw 57 V1 flew for the first time in mid-1936 with Kurt Tank at the controls. Plans called for the addition of two fixed forward-firing 20-mm MG FF cannon in the fuselage nose.

The Henschel Hs 124 was also designed with a powered turret, although in this case it was located in the fuselage nose. The Hs 124 V1 was powered by two Jumo 210 A liquid-cooled engines each producing 610 h.p. The second prototype, the Hs 124 V2, was equipped with more powerful air-cooled BMW 132 engines each producing 870 h.p. The Hs 124 V2 dispensed with the powered

The Henschel Hs 124.

Two photographs of the Fw 57 *Zerstörer*. From the front the Fw 57 was reminiscent of the He 111.

Side view of the very first Messerschmitt Bf 110. The V1 wore no markings when this photograph was taken. (EADS Unternehmensarchiv Ottobrunn via Ebert)

turret, which was replaced by a fully-glazed nose. With a gross weight of 7.2 tons, the V2 nevertheless managed to reach 435 km/h at a height of 3000 meters.

It soon became clear that the three-seat strategic fighter was too heavy and lacking in maneuverability for military purposes. Fully equipped, the Fw 57 weighed almost 8.5 tons, and its maximum speed was an unimpressive 365 km/h. The RLM therefore abandoned the idea of the heavy strategic fighter and instead called for a light, two-seat *Zerstörer* capable of higher speeds. The Bayerische Flugzeugwerke, whose lightweight Bf 110 had stood little chance of satisfying the original heavy *Zerstörer* specification, emerged from this situation as the winner, with virtually no competitors. The Fw 57 and Hs 124 were out of the race.

Dipl.Ing. Hans Sander had very little to do with the testing of the Fw 57, however on one occasion he did make a ferry flight in the aircraft. He found the Fw 57 to be a heavy, unmaneuverable aircraft which was no joy to fly. It is no wonder, then, that development of the Fw 57 was not pursued.

It was solely due to Ernst Udet that the Bf 110 received an RLM contract in the beginning. Prof. Messerschmitt was then aided by the changed profile for the *Kampfzerstörer*. As a result of these changed requirements, especially for a higher maximum speed, the Bf 110 unexpectedly became the front runner and Messerschmitt was instructed to build three prototypes.

The Bf 110 was designed as a stressed-skin low-wing monoplane with a single-spar wing and retractable undercarriage. Its construction was similar to that of the Bf 109 and it was easily identifiable as a member of the Messerschmitt family. The Bf 110 was an aerodynamically clean design with twin fins and rudders to improve the gunner's field of fire.

The first prototype, the Bf 110 V1, flew for the first time on 12 May 1936. Unlike the Fw 187, which came later, from the beginning the Bf 110 V1 was powered by two prototypes of the more powerful Daimler Benz DB 600, a twelve-cylinder inline engine capable of producing 900 h.p. for takeoff. In early test flights the Bf 110 V1 achieved a maximum speed of 510 km/h. The Bf 110 V2 and V3 followed on 24 October and 24 December 1936. In January 1937 the Bf 110 V2 went to the Rechlin test station. The positive results achieved in trials at Rechlin led the RLM to submit an order for four pre-production machines. Test pilots praised the Bf 110 V2's high speed, but criticized its poor maneuverability. What was initially considered a minor shortcoming was to prove disastrous three years later during the Battle of Britain. By 1940 the Bf 110's speed advantage over Allied single-seat fighters had disappeared, and its lack of maneuverability was shown to be a fatal shortcoming. The RLM's decision in favor of the Bf 110 resulted in the cessation of development of all alternatives. Only three Fw 57s were built, while production of the Hs 124 was limited to two prototypes.

Although Focke Wulf's Fw 57 had lost out in the *Zerstörer* competition, soon afterwards the impressive performance of the Fw 187 made a strong impression on some high-ranking officers in the RLM. In spite of the departure of von Richthofen from the *Technische Amt*, a contract was issued to Focke Wulf to continue development of the Fw 187. Focke Wulf must have viewed the Fw 187 as an alternative *Zerstörer*, for in the initial discussions the RLM again had to clarify the mission of the Fw 187. By then the RLM had decided in favor of the Bf 110 for the *Zerstörer* role. The RLM's demands were clear: the Fw 187 would have to be modified for the night fighter role.

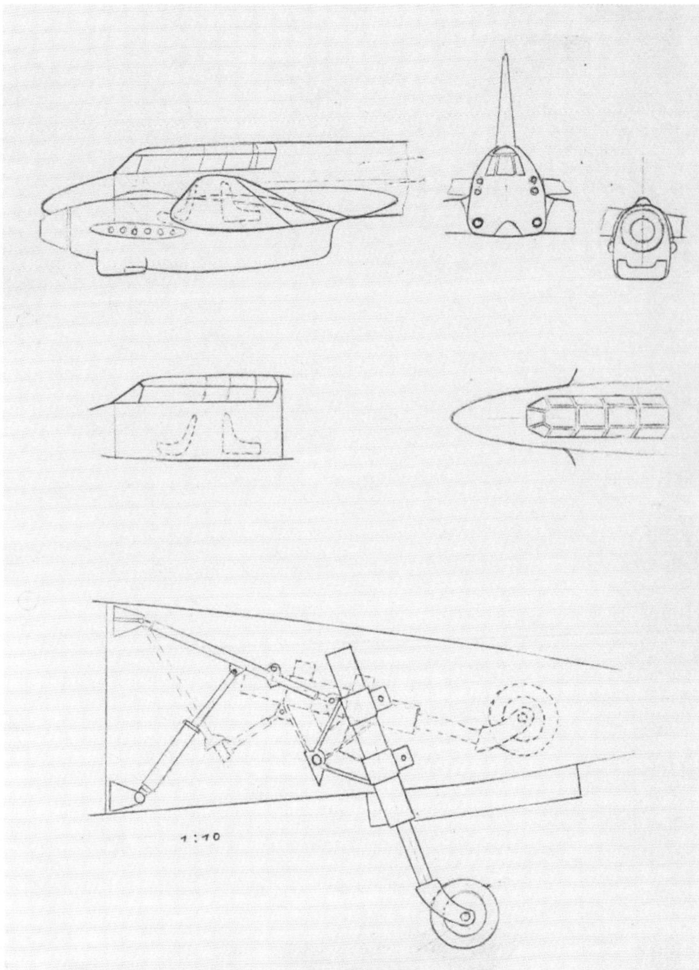

Focke Wulf sketch of the two-seat Fw 187. (EADS Unternehmensarchiv Bremen)

For the night fighter role the Fw 187 would have to be equipped with a second seat, which meant that the entire cockpit area would have to be revised. In December 1937, during a meeting to discuss further development possibilities for the Fw 187, there was an inspection of a mock-up of the two-seat Fw 187. The Fw 187's night fighter was clearly defined for the first time in minutes dated 21 December 1937. The Fw 187 was to become the first German purpose-designed night fighter. Emphasis was placed on the planned electronic equipment and fixed forward-firing armament. Two armament variations were proposed, one with four MG 151 and two MG 204 weapons, and one with two MG 131s and a single MK 301.

The *E-Stelle Rechlin* made a third proposal for an armament of four MG 17 machine-guns and two MG 151 cannon and Focke Wulf was instructed to investigate the feasibility of such an armament. It was decided that each of these armament combinations would be evaluated in pre-production aircraft.

Plans also called for flame dampers for the aircraft's Jumo 210 engines. It was also planned to equip the aircraft with the FuG 10 radio with a fixed antenna. The FuG 10 system consisted of two transmitters, two receivers and the radio control box. To improve range, the antenna mast height was increased by 40 cm. The aircraft's navigational equipment was to include a FuBL 1 instrument landing aid.

The Fw 187 A-0 Pre-production Series is Built as a Heavy Fighter

Although plans had existed to build a pre-production series of the Fw 187 single-seat variant, no type designation was assigned. The RLM had lost interest in a single-seat Fw 187 very quickly and was obsessed with the *Zerstörer* concept, a two-seat twin-engined heavy fighter. The RLM also preferred the two-seat version of the Fw 187. In spite of tremendous efforts by Focke Wulf, neither the single- or two seat version of the Fw 187 entered production in 1937. The RLM also quickly lost interest in the night fighter version of the Fw 187. The only action it took was to issue a pre-production contract for a heavy fighter version of the Fw 187, which technically lay somewhere between the Messerschmitt Bf 109 and Bf 110. The *Luftwaffe*'s interest in this class of warplane was actually very limited. With the awarding of an official RLM contract, the new two-seat series was designated the Fw 187 A-0. The question was whether this new variant of the Fw 187 would demonstrate a sufficiently impressive performance.

The prototype of the new Fw 187 A series was the Fw 187 V4 (RLM contract number 10 07 038). Beginning with the Fw 187 V4, the RLM ordered just five additional pre-production aircraft, all of which were completed. When the Fw 187 V4 was completed, new Focke Wulf test pilot Kurt Mehlhorn assumed sole responsibility for its testing. According to chief test pilot Hans Sander, testing lasted from 27 October 1938 to 6 February 1939. The V4, whose serial number was 1966, was assigned the civil registration D-ORHP.

Impressive photograph of a Fw 187 A-0 with engines running. (Focke Wulf)

D-OSNP takes off on another test flight. (Focke Wulf)

The V4 was used to extensively test the Fw 187's hydraulic systems and for trials with VDM variable-pitch propellers. As well, it was supposed to be the first to employ Schwarz shrouded wooden propellers. Although the V4 was supposed to be tested at Rechlin, to date there is no direct proof that the aircraft actually went there. According to information provided by Hans Sander, Kurt Mehlhorn made the last flight in the Fw 187 V4. An engine caught fire and the pilot landed the aircraft on its belly. The damage was not repaired, and after technical tests the disassembled V4 was handed back to the RLM on 10 September 1939. It appears that some parts were returned, however, for as late as March 1945 Focke Wulf undertook performance measurements on the tail section of the Fw 187.

Focke Wulf completed five more Fw 197 A-0s corresponding to RLM contracts 10 07 039 and 10 07 040. The aircraft serial numbers were 1967, 1968, 1969, 1974 and 1975. With the exception of 1967, which was transferred disassembled to the RLM on 23 September 1939, all of these aircraft participated in various test programs. For example, in July 1939 *Werknummer* 1968 was being used by Argus for undercarriage tests in Berlin-Schönefeld. Werner Stege was among the pilots who flew D-OVRB in June-July 1939. Shortly before the outbreak of war *Werknummer* 1969, registration D-OTGN, was assigned to Rheinmetall-Borsig. On 23 October 1939 test pilot Erich Bieneck flew the aircraft from Bremen to Fassberg, where weapons trials were to be carried out for the *E-Stelle Rechlin*. No details of these trials have survived. On completion of trials, D-

In contrast to the original seat position, here the pilot and radio operator sit one behind the other in the cockpit of the Fw 187 A-0. (Focke Wulf)

Impressive photograph of Yellow 7, a Fw 187 A-0, in inverted flight over northern Germany. (Focke Wulf)

OTGN was flown back to Bremen by Erich Bieneck on 8 May 1940. At that time *Werknummer* 1974 was being flown by the *E-Stelle Rechlin*. At that time all of the Fw 187s carried a standard armament of two MG 17 machine-guns and two MG 151 cannon. The rearward-firing MG 81 was not installed, however. Only later was the armament converted to two MG 17s and two MG FF cannon.

At a later date all A-0 machines were fitted with a revised windscreen suitable for combat operations. It incorporated a prominent armor-glass windscreen and flat triangular panels. One of the last three zero-series machines, *Werknummer* 1974, was converted into the Fw 187 V6. In spite of the new prototype number, the only difference between the V6 and the other zero-series aircraft was its strengthened armament. Two MG 17s replaced the single machine-gun on each side of the fuselage, and the most prominent change was the bulged fairings over the weapons. The V6 was also the first to receive the new armored windscreen.

The new armament caused no problems and the revised windscreen also proved a success. All A-0 aircraft were subsequently modified to this standard.

Fw 187 V4 and Zero-Series Specifications[1]

General

The Fw 187 V4 was developed from the earlier Fw 187 V1 to V3 prototypes.

In keeping with its design role of heavy fighter, emphasis was placed on maneuverability, speed and rate of climb. Unlike the Fw 187 V1 to V3, the V4 was designed to accommodate a crew of two. The aircraft's powerful armament makes it suitable for both offensive and defensive roles.

The large fuel capacity gives the aircraft the endurance required for defensive patrols. Endurance at reduced power (33%) is 6.15 hours at an altitude of 4 500 meters and speed of 375 km/h.

The aircraft will be most effective in the bomber escort role by suppressing the enemy's defenses. As the aircraft's role will expose it to enemy fire, the fuel tanks have been provided with medium lightweight armor. The second crew member will ease the pilot's workload by operating the radio and by scanning and defending aft. For rearwards defense, which is especially important in dog-

[1] The forward fuselage contains the rudder pedals and mounts. In the nose are fittings for the mounting of a machine-gun camera. On the underside of the forward fuselage is a large, easily removable glazed panel. The section ends in an oblique end frame in front of the instrument panel. The forward fuselage is attached by bolts to the fuselage center-section.

The V4 was the first example of the Fw 187 two-seat *Zerstörer* and as such the direct predecessor of the planned production variant.

Two company photographs of the Fw 187 V4 under construction.

fighting, the observer is provided with a flexibly-mounted MG 81 with 1,000 rounds.

In addition to the standard emergency lighting, the aircraft is equipped with a FS 130a searchlight system, which installed in the port wing.

I. Fuselage

Constructed of Dural, the stressed skin fuselage is made up of four components which are manufactured separately. These components are assembled in the following order:

1.) Forward fuselage
2.) Fuselage center-section
3.) Rear fuselage
4.) Fuselage tail section with tail cone

2.) The fuselage center-section incorporates the cockpit, which is forward of the wing, the observer's compartment, which is in the area of the wing, the radio equipment, the ammunition boxes, and the fuselage tanks. The fuselage center-section and rear fuselage meet just aft of the wing root filet. The fuselage center-section consists of a bottom shell, two side shells and a canopy which extends far enough to the rear to provide the rearwards-facing observer with a good field of view. The canopy, which is made of Plexiglas, is in two parts, with the front section folding forward and the rear section folding aft. The junction of the two sections, at roughly the midway point, is designed in such a way that the forward section overlaps the rear, thus preventing lifting by the slipstream.

In an emergency both sections can be jettisoned by means of a jettisoning handle easily reached by either crew member, making it possible for both cockpits to be exited without hindrance. The firing tubes for the MG 151 are armored with 3-mm sheet steel from the wing leading edge to where they exit the forward fuselage.

Access to the upper and central weapons (2 or 4 MG 17s) is provided by side panels, while the lower weapons (2 MG 151 or 2 MG FF cannon) are accessible from the observer's position. A cutout in the underside of the fuselage center-section accommodates the one-piece wing center-section.

Cockpit of the Fw 187 V4. The pilot's instrumentation was centrally arranged and designed for readability. The floor window further improved the pilot's view.

The radio operator's seat faced aft. Some equipment remains to be installed in the rear cockpit. (Focke Wulf)

3.) In the bottom of the rear fuselage there is an access panel which provides access to the oxygen bottles, which are located immediately aft of the end frame, and the instrument landing system, which is housed in the fuselage center-section between the bottles.

The access panel also allows entry into the fuselage for the purpose of attaching the fuselage tail section or tail cone. The fuselage sections are attached to one another by bolts.

A ladder which retracts with the undercarriage enables the crew to climb onto the wing and then into the cockpit.

4.) The fuselage tail section, consisting of the shell beneath the horizontal stabilizer and the tail cone, together with the vertical stabilizer, is attached to the rear fuselage by bolts. The retractable tailwheel is housed in the bottom shell of the tail section. The retraction mechanism and the tailwheel mounts, plus the controls in the tail section, are accessible by means of panels in the shell and the removable tail cone.

Fuselage arrangement: the pilot's seat is similar in shape and mounting to the latest Focke Wulf adjustable seat. The seat adjustment range is 100 mm and is designed so that the selected pedal distance remains constant. The adjusting lever is on the right side facing aft. The seat is equipped with a swiveling backrest which makes it possible for the strapped-in pilot to turn his upper body.

The backrest of the observer's seat rests against the ammunition boxes for the upper and central weapons. It folds to provide maintenance access to the equipment located beneath. No adjustment is planned. The observer is restrained by a standard lap belt.

II. Undercarriage

1.) The undercarriage consists of two identical units which are accommodated in undercarriage gondolas aft of the engines. The undercarriage legs are interchangeable without modification.

The selected wheels are Argus brake-wheels with 815x290 tires. The wheels are equipped with hydraulic brakes. Shock absorption is provided by VDM air oleos which form part of a rigid frame. Each frame is braced aft by two folding retraction struts.

Retraction of the undercarriage is accomplished by two hydraulic retraction cylinders which operate in unison with accumulators mounted parallel to the retraction struts.

The hydraulic pressure needed to retract the undercarriage is provided by two axial pumps mounted on the engines. Should one pump fail, the entire system automatically switches to the remaining serviceable pump.

Extension is hydraulic, supported by the accumulators. In the event of an hydraulic failure, it is possible to lower the undercarriage at speeds up to 200 km/h by gravity assisted by the accumulators.

Indicator lights indicate the undercarriage end positions, with red for "EXTENDED" and green for "RETRACTED". Warning indications are provided by a Bosch horn and flashing light.

The undercarriage gondola fairings consist of:

a) Two (left and right) supporting shells, in which the undercarriage pivots are mounted. From the pivots to the end of the gondola the fairings consist of normal metal skinning.

b) Two undercarriage doors.

c) The gondola end piece, which is attached to the wing flap, and which telescopes into the undercarriage gondola as the undercarriage is retracted.

Tailwheel bay.

2.) The tailwheel has an EC wheel with inflatable tire (380x150). Shock absorption is provided by an EC leg (oil-damped steel spring) which is incorporated into the retraction strut. A return mechanism places the tailwheel in the central position when the aircraft leaves the ground. The entire tailwheel system is housed in the removable shell portion of the tail section, making it possible to assemble the tailwheel and its retraction mechanism outside the aircraft. Once installed, the tailwheel is accessible by means of access panels and the easily-removed tail cone. The tailwheel is retracted hydraulically together with the main undercarriage. Extension of the tailwheel is accomplished by an accumulator and gravity and may thus be extended even after a failure of the hydraulic system.

In the retracted position the tailwheel projects from the tailwheel doors by approximately 10 cm and may be employed as a tail skid. The tailwheel bay is covered by sprung doors.

III. Control Surfaces

1. Tailplane

The tailplane is a one-piece, all-metal stressed-skin structure which is bolted to the fuselage shell and vertical fin. The elevator is in two parts which are joined by a shaft. The elevator halves are interchangeable.

The control surface consists of a metal-covered torsion nose with end ribs. The remainder of the surface is fabric covered. The elevator is aerodynamically balanced by means of a horn and compensating flaps in the leading edge. The compensating flaps operate automatically as the control surface is deflected and may also be set manually from the cockpit for trimming. The elevator is directly mass balanced.

2. Fin and Rudder

The fin and the fuselage section above the tailplane are produced as a single stressed-skin component. It is joined to the tailplane and bottom fuselage shell by flange bolts. The fin consists of three spars, longitudinal members and frames with metal skinning.

The rudder consists of a metal-covered torsion nose with end ribs and fabric covering. It is directly mass-balanced. Aerodynamic balance is achieved by an automatically-controlled compensating flap in the leading edge of the rudder. The flap may also be set manually from the cockpit for trimming.

3. Ailerons

Each aileron consists of an outer and inner section. When the split flaps are lowered the inner sections act as landing flaps.

The ailerons consist of a metal-skinned torsion nose with end ribs and fabric covering. The ailerons are directly mass balanced.

Fw 187 tailwheel.

Aerodynamic balance is achieved by the nose shape and automatic compensating flaps in the leading edge. The compensating flap in the port aileron may also be set manually from the cockpit for trimming.

4. Split Flaps

The split flaps are covered with metal skinning on the bottom and stiffened by ribs and longitudinal members. They extend from the wing root filet across the end piece of the undercarriage gondola to the wing junction. The end pieces of the undercarriage gondolas are attached to the split flaps and telescope into the gondolas when the flaps are retracted.

Assembly of the Fw 187 A-0. Note the fuselage cutout for installation of the MG 17. (Focke Wulf)

IV. Control Elements

Control is achieved by a conventional control stick using cables and pushrods. The stick is mounted on the seat, so that its relative height does not change when the seat position is adjusted.

Standard rudder pedals are used. Beneath the pedals, which may also be adjusted in flight, is the hydraulic cylinder for the wheel brakes. Braking is controlled by toe pressure.

The ailerons have a deflection of 62 degrees. When the split flaps are lowered (60 degree deflection), the inner ailerons are also deflected hydraulically.

V. Wing

The wing is a cantilever structure and consists of a center-section and two outer wing panels. With the exception of elliptical wingtips, the wing outline consists of straight lines. The leading edge of the inner wing is perpendicular to the fuselage axis. The leading edges of the outer wings are swept at 4 degrees with 6 degrees of dihedral. For construction reasons, the outer wings are divided into upper and lower shells.

1.) Located on the top of the **wing center-section** at the wing root is a flange for connection to the fuselage. After assembly, this bolt flange is covered by the wing root fairing. At each end of the center-section there is an engine nacelle.

The leading edge of the wing between the fuselage and engine nacelles folds for easy access to control rods and lines.

The wing center-section is a four-spar structure, with spars 1, 2 and 3 being continuous elements. The box spar formed by spars 1 and 2 is essentially a torsion tube which is only interrupted by spaces for the ammunition boxes and oil tanks. The fuel tanks are located in the area between spars 2 and 3, between the engine nacelles and the fuselage, while the ammunition boxes and radio operator's seat

Servicing the engines of a Fw 187 A-0. (Focke Wulf)

are in the fuselage. Spar 4 is interrupted in the area of the fuselage on account of the fuselage fuel tank. Additional ammunition boxes for the MG 151s are located in the wing behind spar 3.

Split flaps are situated on the trailing edge from the wing junction to the fuselage.

2.) The **outer wings** are built around three spars and are split into upper and lower shells.

The shells are attached to the spars with screws and can easily be removed during overhaul or repair, making all areas easily accessible. Mounted in the outer wings are two-piece ailerons. The outer wings are attached to the center-section by bolts along the end ribs and spars. The wing junctions are covered by metal strips.

VI. Power Plants

The aircraft is powered by two Jumo 210 G engines, for which a performance summary follows:

Speed at n = 2,700 rpm.	
H = 0 m	N = 700 h.p.
H = 3 900 m	N = 670 h.p.
H = 4 600 m	N = 605 h.p.
Propeller reduction ratio	1 : 1.75
Liquid cooling	t = 95C
Heat to be dispersed	
on ground	222 000 WE/h
fuel-injected engine	

It is possible to install the Jumo 210 F, however this required modifications to the engine mounts in the area of the engine accessories and radiator mounts.

1.) Engine Mounts

The engines are mounted in bearers with an open U-profile of 2.5-mm sheet steel. The forward attachment points are mounted in bearing boxes, the rear in rubber mounts.

2.) Engine Cowlings

The nacelles are divided into engine cowling and undercarriage gondola by a vertical partition, roughly in the area of the engine accessories. The partition is designed in such a way as to ventilate the engine compartment. The cowling is attached to the engine at the partition.

Junkers Jumo 210 G engine with motor mounts, ready for installation in the Fw 187 A airframe. (EADS Unternehmensarchiv Bremen)

The engine cowling consists of:

a) A removable upper section.

b) Two side panels, left and right, which provide access to the spark-plugs and exhaust flange. The inner side panels house the required engine instruments.

c) The radiator fairing, which is attached to the exhaust flange by four screws and which can easily be removed from below. The panel built into the radiator fairing provides access to the injection pumps.

d) A rear side panel, which provides access to the lower accessory bay. The upper part of the accessory bay is accessible by means of a panel in the fairing above the wing.

e) The left and right exhaust pipes. The intake shaft for the super-charger is located in the fairing above the wing.

Firewall

The engine compartment is separated from the undercarriage gondola and the wing by a firewall. The firewall extends from the bottom of Spar 1 to the undercarriage pivots and is made up of: 0.5 mm Dural, 0.8 mm Reinz fabric, 2 mm Reinz fabric, 1 mm Dural.

3.) Propellers

VDM three-blade, variable-pitch propellers with a diameter of 3.1 meters. There is an opening at the front of the spinner for ventilation of the engine compartment. The cooling air flows out through the partition between the engine and undercarriage fairings. If necessary, exit slots could be placed in front of the firewall.

4.) Ignition System

A Bosch SKH inertia starter with hand drive is used.

To ease startup on the ground, the hand crank axes were arranged in line with the undercarriage pivot axes and interconnected by a window chain.

Engine start is accomplished with a hand crank manufactured by Focke Wulf. An adapter is provided so that the standard Bosch hand crank may also be used.

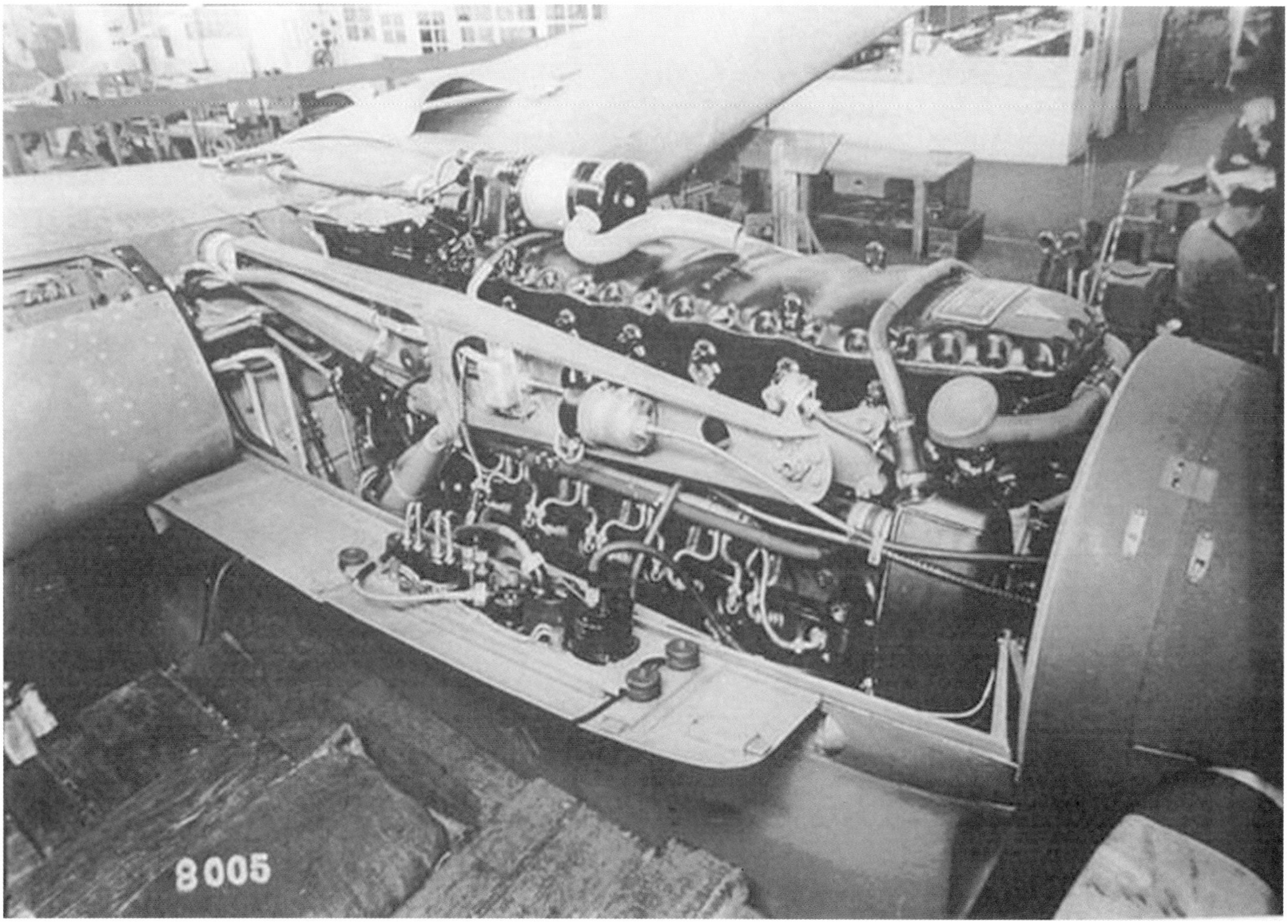

Jumo engine installation in the Fw 187 V4. (Focke Wulf)

5.) Exhaust System
The ejector port system is provided by Junkers. To avoid blinding the pilot (while reading the engine instruments) a shield is mounted above the ejector ports.

6.) Engine Hoses and Lines
Pantal hoses and Maximall fittings are used. Exhaust hoses are located in the engine compartment. The location of fuel and oil lines may be seen in drawings 18700-7551 and 752. The lines in the wing center-section and fuselage are rigidly mounted.

7.) Cooling System
The radiator is situated on the underside of the engine. It is planned to include an equalizing valve in the cooling circuit, which is based on the shunt principle. The shunt installation is located in front of the coolant pump. For a schematic of the cooling system see drawing No. 18700-753. The cooling air intake is non-adjustable. It is planned to add an adjustable flap in the cooling air outlet. Powered by an electric motor, the flap will be controlled by an electric hand switch. Should the electric motor fail, the pilot can open the cooling flap from the cockpit by means of a control rod. The oil cooler is mounted on the bottom left side of the engine. Cooling air is fed into the cooler by an intake scoop in the radiator fairing.

8.) Linkage
The linkage is designed to be visible and easily accessible. Weaknesses and excessively high control forces have been carefully avoided. DUZ pipe has been used where a normal linkage could not be used.

9.) Tanks
There are three fuel tanks and two oil tanks. All tanks are provided with medium lightweight armor.

10.) Lubrication System
Two oil tanks, each with a capacity of 48 liters, are located in the undercarriage gondolas aft of the firewall in the area between Spars 1 and 2.

TV 6 bleeder valves are installed in the oil tanks. The oil lines are connected at the bottom of the tanks by special attachment

The Fw 187 A had three fuel tanks, which were held in place by straps. (EADS Unternehmensarchiv Bremen)

Damaged fuel tank in the wing of a Fw 187.

Fuselage cross-section of the Fw 187 showing the attachment points. The triangular cross-section is reminiscent of that of the Me 262 jet fighter. (EADS Unternehmensarchiv Bremen)

flanges. With oil lines to and from the engines, it is possible to switch on an engine pump to circulate warm oil through the engine.

If an engine is lost, a pumping system makes it possible to transfer the oil from the dead engine to the remaining serviceable engine.

11.) Fuel System

Three fuel tanks are provided. Two are located in the wing center-section, left and right, between Ribs 2 and 6, while the third is situated in the fuselage between Frames 11 and 15. Each wing tank has a capacity of 245 liters, the fuselage tank 620 liters. The tank compartments are isolated by bulkheads.

Fuel is only drawn from the fuselage tank. Fuel from the wing tanks is fed into the fuselage tank by two EP 1 electric pump units. A return line ensures that excess fuel returns to the wing tanks. Ventilation takes place only through the wing tanks. The switch for the EP 1 system is coupled with the fuel cock.

The covers beneath the fuel tanks contain holes to allow any lost fuel to drain. The holes are covered with a thin rubber skin which dissolves when moistened by fuel.

A fuel hand pump is located in the leading edge of the wing between the nacelle and the fuselage. The pump for the injection tank is located in the engine nacelle.

In the fuselage tank there is a tank pump which delivers fuel to the engines at higher altitudes. A placard in the cockpit tells the pilot at which altitude to switch on the pump.

Removing a tarpaulin from the Jumo 210 engine of a Fw 187 A-0. (Focke Wulf)

Equipment

The height of the main instrument panel has been limited in order to avoid restricting the pilot's view over the fuselage nose and below through the window in the floor. It was therefore necessary to install auxiliary panels on both sides of the cockpit. The radio operator is also provided with an instrument panel. Among the systems housed in the auxiliary panels are the ignition switches, sensitivity control for the turn-and-bank indicator, electrical system cutout switch, flare pistol, signal cartridges and oxygen equipment.

The ammunition boxes for the four upper fuselage weapons were arranged between the seats, as in the cockpit of *Werknummer* 1974. The four compressed-air bottles were used to charge the machine-guns. (Focke Wulf)

1.) Flight and Navigation Instruments
Both the pilot's and observer's instrument panels contain altimeter, airspeed indicator, clock and compass.

2.) Engine Instruments
The instruments for each engine are placed in the side of the engine nacelle facing the pilot. They are arranged in small panels and are easily visible to the pilot from the cockpit. To avoid blinding the pilot (while reading the engine instruments) a shield is mounted above the ejector ports.

3.) Identification Equipment
A flare pistol is housed in the right auxiliary panel within reach of the pilot. The associated flare cartridge box is on the right side of the cockpit.

Photographed during final assembly, the rather prominent antenna mast of the Fw 187. (Focke Wulf)

The original armament of the Fw 187 A-0 consisted of a pair of MG 17 machine-guns and two MG 151 cannon. Ammunition for the two MG 17s was fed from boxes between the pilot's and radio operator's seats. One ammunition box is open in this photograph.

Two views of the cockpit of the Fw 187 V4. (Focke Wulf)

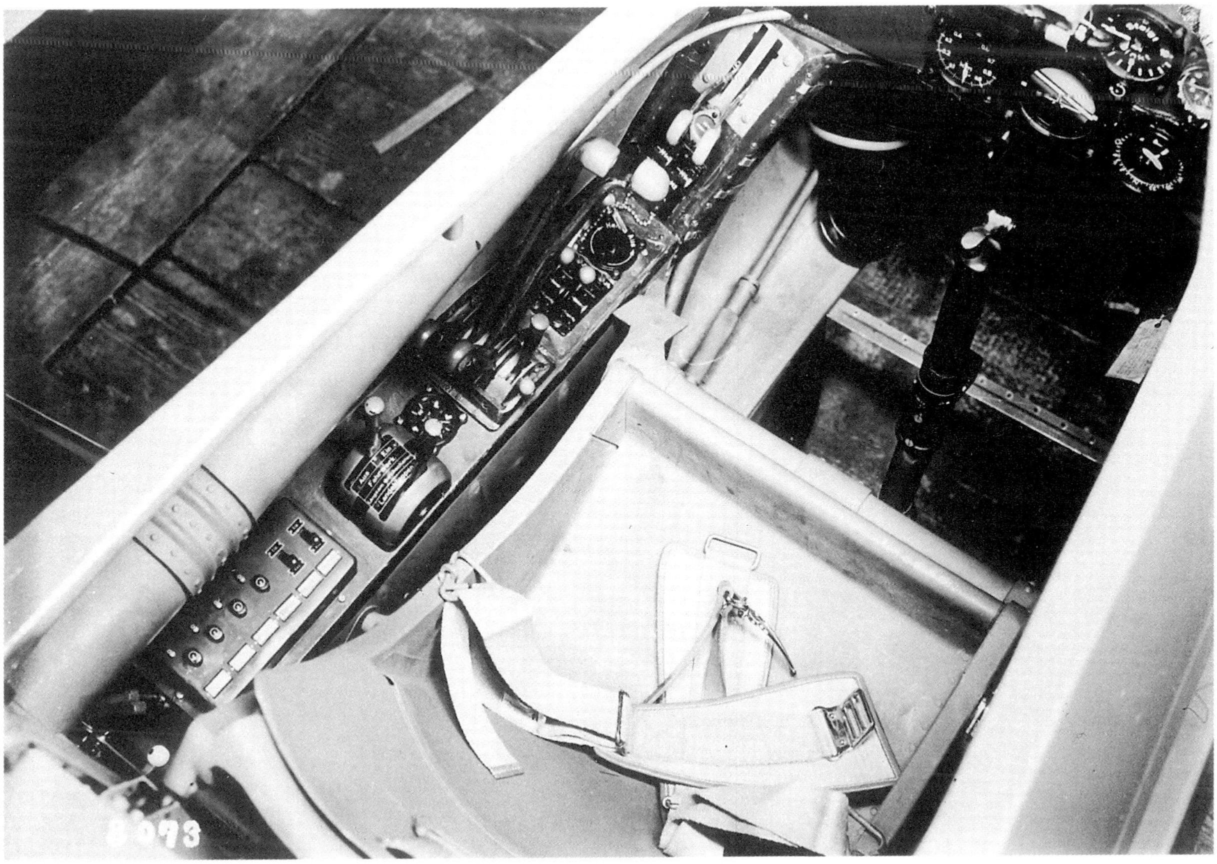

The radio equipment installed in the rear cockpit of the Fw 187. This photograph was taken facing aft. (Focke Wulf)

4.) Radio Equipment

Radio equipment consists of an FuG X with fixed antenna for signals and command transmission and an FuBl 1 instrument landing system. The FuG X is situated in the radio operator's compartment in front of Frame 13 within easy reach of the radio operator. The FuBl 1 is located in the rear fuselage just behind the junction (Frame 15/16).

5.) Safety Equipment

Both the pilot and radio operator are provided with gas masks and oxygen equipment. The light metal oxygen bottles are stowed in the rear fuselage right next to the junction (Frame 15/16). Near them is a first-aid kit. While the pilot's seat is equipped with shoulder and lap belts, the radio operator's seat has only a lap belt. The shoulder belt was dispensed with in order to provide maximum freedom of movement while operating the MG 81.

6.) Electrical System

A Bosch generator located on the port engine delivers 1,200 Watts at an operating voltage of 24 V. The Varta 12 G1 3 battery (20 Amp.) is also located in the port engine nacelle, between the engine and the firewall.

7.) Tool Kit

The tool kit is located in the aft fuselage.

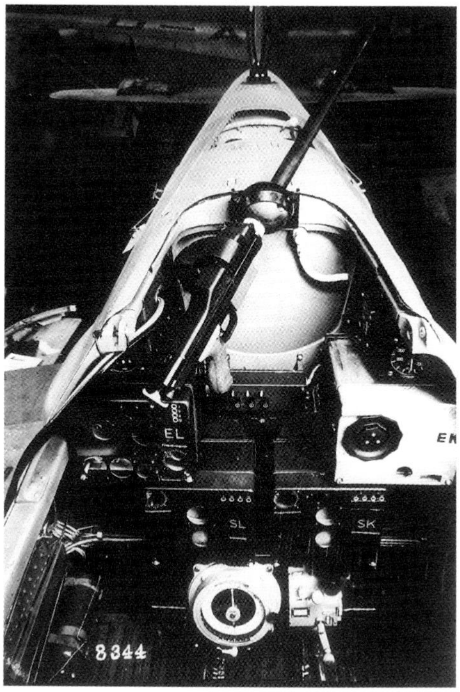

Radio operator's cockpit with radio equipment and rearward-firing MG 81. The MG 81 was provided with 1,000 rounds of ammunition and had a range of movement of 15-60 degrees vertically and 30 degrees horizontally (to each side). (Focke Wulf)

View of the staggered MG 17 machine-guns with access panel removed. This heavier armament was installed at a later date. (Focke Wulf)

Armament

The aircraft can be equipped with four fixed and one movable weapon or six fixed and one flexible weapon. The following armament combinations are possible:

I. 2 MG 17 (1,000 round per gun), 2 MG FF (60 round per gun) and 1 MG 81 (1,000 rounds).
II. 2 MG 17 (1,000 round per gun), 2 MG 151 (280 round per gun) and 1 MG 81 (1,000 rounds).
III. 4 MG 17 (1,000 round per gun), 2 MG 151 (600 round per gun) and 1 MG 81 (1,000 rounds).

The fixed weapons are housed in the fuselage, one above the other in the fuselage sides above the wing. Removable panels provide easy access to the guns. The weapons themselves are mounted in such a way that they can be removed without resighting.

The fixed weapons are fired by means of the KG 12a control grip. Planned aiming device is the Revi 12c. The cocking buttons are on the left side of the main instrument panel.

All ammunition boxes, with the exception of those in the wing, can easily be removed. Belts of ammunition are loaded into the wing boxes through hatches on the upper surface of the wing.

The two MG 151s are situated in the fuselage sidewalls just above the floor. Two ammunition boxes are located in the fuselage, with two more in the wing between Spars 3 and 4. The firing tubes are armored with 3-mm tempered steel sheet to protect the pilot in the event a shell should detonate prematurely (see Fuselage Center-Section). In the other armament combination two MG FF cannon may be installed in place of the MG 151s. Cocking is pneumatic. Ammunition is housed in 60-round drums attached directly to the weapons.

Located above the cannon are one or two MG 17s. They are equipped with an electro-pneumatic cocking mechanism. The necessary compressed air bottles are located above the ammunition boxes.

The MG 81 is located in the fuselage center-section above Frame 13. It is operated by the radio operator and has a range of movement of 15°-60° vertically and 30° horizontally to the left and right. The weapon's purpose is to defend against attacks from the rear and is especially suited to dogfighting. 1,000 rounds of ammunition are carried for this weapon.

Two interesting close-ups illustrating the two different armament combinations installed in the fuselage sides of the Fw 187 A-0. The photo above depicts the staggered twin MG 17 installation. The installation of a total of four MG 17s was considered to place the aircraft in an overloaded condition. The photograph below depicts the original installation with a single MG 17 on each side. Visible in the bottom photograph is the original bulged windscreen, which was replaced by a new framed windscreen with flat armor glass panels. (Focke Wulf)

Fw 187 V4 and 0-Series Specification

Spec. Sheet No. 131

Type:	Fw 187 0-Series
Wing area:	30.20 m^2
Wingspan:	15.48 m
Maximum height:	3.85 m
Maximum length:	11.20 m
Engines:	Jumo 210 G
Engine output:	675 h.p. at 2,700 rpm at height of 4600 m
Propeller speed:	1,543 rpm
Propellers:	3-blade metal variable-pitch, diameter 3.1 m

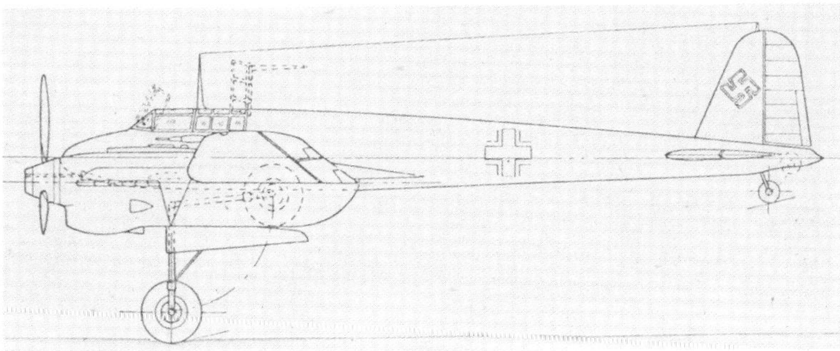

Specification sheet for the Fw 187 A-0 with Jumo 210 G engines and a gross weight of 5000 kg.

Performance at gross weight of 5000 kg:

Maximum speed at	0 m	466 km/h
	1900 m	515 km/h
	2900 m	507 km/h
	4600 m	545 km/h
	5000 m	541 km/h
	6000 m	528 km/h
Rate of climb at ground level	12.1 m/sec	
Time to climb	0 ñ 2000 m	2.8 min.
	0 ñ 4000 m	6.2 min.
	0 ñ 6000 m	10.4 min.
Service ceiling	10000 m	
Landing speed	130 km/h	
Endurance at full throttle at 4600 m		2.7 hr.
Range		1450 km

The maximum speeds were calculated taking into consideration the increase in maximum boost altitude by taking advantage of dynamic pressure and the increase in performance produced by exhaust energy. The following information provided by Junkers was used in calculating maximum speed:

1.) Maximum boost altitude raised from 3900 to 4500 meters by exploiting dynamic pressure.

2.) Engine performance increased by 13% as a result of exhaust thrust.

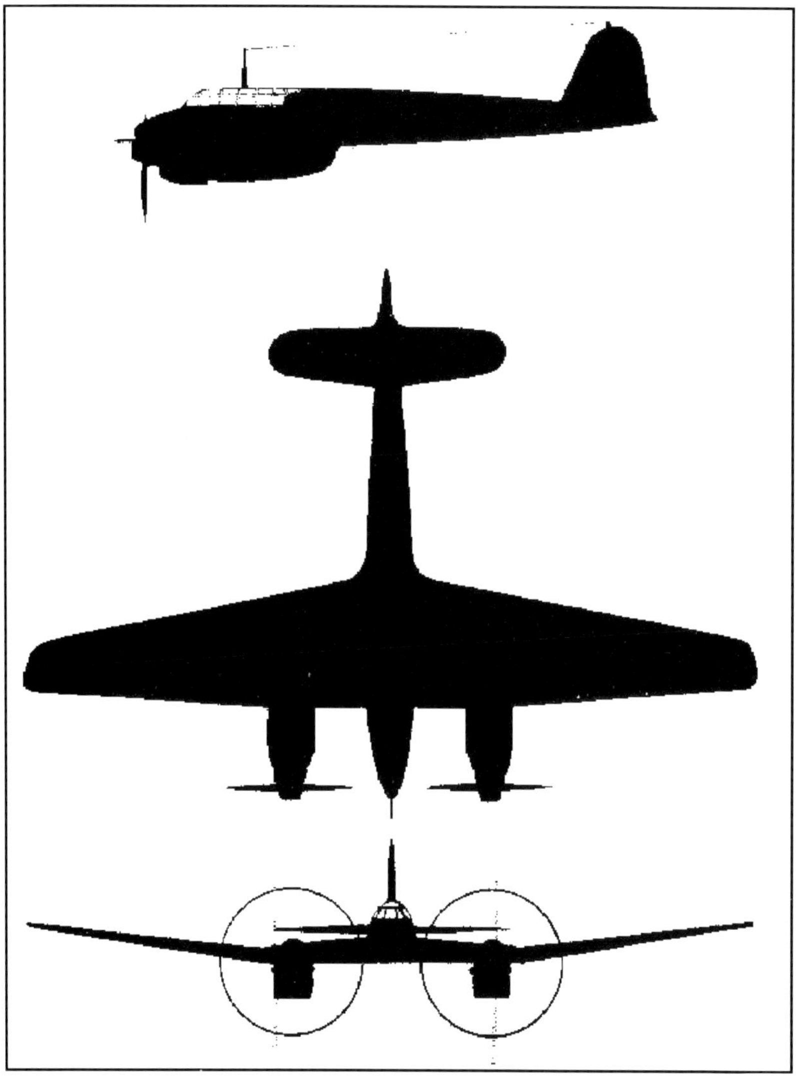

Three-view silhouette of the Fw 187 A.

Retouched photograph of the Fw 187 V4 for the aircraft handbook.

This accident involving the Fw 187 V4 resulted in the entire undercarriage being ripped away. It is thought that test pilot Kurt Mehlhorn was flying the aircraft. Evidence suggests that the forced-landing was caused by a fire in the starboard engine.

Summary of Costs for the Fw 187 V4 and Fw 187 A-0

The summary of costs for the Fw 187 V4 and the five A-0 pre-production aircraft has survived intact. It contains a precise record of all contract and completion dates. Focke Wulf received the contract to build the Fw 187 V4 (RLM contract no. 10 07 038) on 9 March 1938. A total of 100,578.60 man hours as required to construct the V4. This corresponded to 105,922 RM (*Reichsmark*) in wages. Material costs for the Fw 187 V4 totaled 89,211.47 RM.

Production of the Zero-Series proceeded more quickly. The next summary of costs for the first two pre-production aircraft, *Werknummer* 1967 and 1968 (Contract 10 07 039), revealed material costs of 150,795.54 RM, or 75,397.77 RM per aircraft. Wage costs totaled 155,420.57 RM for 146,727.25 man hours, which equates to 77,710.29 RM and 73,373.63 man hours for each machine. The cost summary for the last three Fw 187 A-0s is dated 22 January 1940 (Contract 10 07 040). Material costs alone for the construction of the three Fw 187 A-0s with the *Werknummer* 1969, 1974 and 1975 were 224,323.39 RM. To this was added 204,409.23 RM in labor costs for 193,468.85 man hours. This equates to 74,774.46 RM in materials and 63,136.41 RM in labor costs for 64,489.62 man hours for each Fw 187 A-0. A comparison of these figures reveals that material costs and construction time per machine, and therefore wage costs, dropped steadily as production went on.

Just how detailed these summaries were in those days is revealed by the fact that they were up to 41 pages long. Each component was examined, listed and calculated. An example is Component 202, undercarriage with VDM shock strut and 710x220 Argus wheel. The total time required for the three Fw 187 A-0 aircraft was 3,749.2 hours. Wage costs were 4,224.98 RM and material costs 19,466.74 RM.

D-OTGN, *Werknummer* 1969, was another A-0 series aircraft. (Focke Wulf)

Two in-flight photographs of the Fw 187 A-0. (Focke Wulf)

Two excellent close-ups of a Fw 187 A-0, probably *Werknummer* 1967. The engine instruments in the nacelle are clearly visible. Note the color-coded rings around the instruments which identified the systems they served. (Sengfelder)

Performance Compairson Between the Fw 187 V4 and the Bf 110 B-0

While series production of the Bf 110 was getting under way, Focke Wulf was still hoping for a production contract for the Fw 187. production of the improved Bf 110 B began in March 1938. In order to obtain a more accurate picture of the Fw 187 A-0's performance, the following comparison was made with the improved Bf 110 B. The two *Zerstörer* designs were created at the same time and both were powered by the Junkers Jumo 210 G. From a performance standpoint, therefore, both machines started out largely equal. In terms of weight the Fw 187 possessed a number of advantages resulting from its design. The Fw 187 was 800 kg lighter than the Bf 110. This was of course reflected in the Focke Wulf's better performance. It was 86 km/h faster than the Bf 110 at low level and 90 km/h faster at maximum boost altitude. These impressive figures were totally ignored by the RLM.

Designation:	Focke Wulf Fw 187 V4	Messerschmitt Bf 110 B-0
Purpose	Two-seat fighter/*Zerstörer*	Two-seat *Zerstörer*
Empty weight	3 402 kg	4 440 kg
Gross weight	4 900 kg	5 701 kg
Wingspan	15.48 m	16.16 m
Length	11.20 m	12.60 m
Height	3.85 m	3.48 m
Wing area	30.20 m^2	38.55 m^2
Wing loading	165.56 kg/m^2	147.88 kg/m^2
Power plants	2 x Jumo 210 G	2 x Jumo 210 Ga
Takeoff power	2 x 700 PS	2x700PS
Fuel	B 4	B4
Maximum capacity	1110 l (620 l + 2 x 245 l)	1270 l
Range	1450 km	635 km
Takeoff distance	154 m	400 m
Speed at low level	466 km/h	380 km/h
Maximum speed	545 km/h	455 km/h
at maximum boost altitude	4 600 m	4 000 m
Rate of climb at low level	12.10 m/s	12.50 m/s
Service ceiling	10000m	8000m
Fuselage armament	12 x 20 mm MG FF, 2 x 7.92 mm MG 17 and 1 x MG 81	2x20mmMG FF, 4x7.92mm MG 17 and 1 x MG 15

In 1938 the Bf 110 B was a contemporary of the Fw 187 A. This version equipped the first *Zerstörergruppen*. The performance of the Messerschmitt aircraft was significantly inferior to that of the Fw 187. (EADS Unternehmensarchiv Ottobrunn via Ebert)

The Fw 187 was also superior in range. Only in overloaded condition was the Bf 110 B capable of extending its range to 1220 km, and this was achieved at the cost of performance. The Bf 110's standard armament was heavier than that of the Fw 187 by two MG 17s. In overloaded condition, however, at a gross weight of 5,300 kg, the Fw 187 was capable of carrying a heavier armament of four MG 17s and two MG FF cannon. Even in this configuration it was still 400 kg lighter than the Bf 110 B.

A total of 45 examples of the Bf 110 B was built before production was switched to the improved Bf 110 C. The B-series machines were issued to three newly-formed *Zerstörergruppen*, I./LG 1, I./ZG 1 and I./ZG 76. These first Bf 110s formed the foundation for the later *Zerstörer* units of the *Luftwaffe* and were therefore used mainly for training crews and technical personnel.

Although testing of the previously-described Fw 187 V4, the later Fw 187 V6 and the subsequent Fw 187 A-0 pre-production aircraft produced positive results, the RLM informed Focke Wulf and its chief designer Kurt Tank that it had decided on the Bf 110 as the *Luftwaffe*'s future *Zerstörer*. For years Kurt Tank and the company had tried to awaken the RLM's interest in the Fw 187, however all their efforts had been in vain. Focke Wulf was forced to accept the RLM's decision against series production of the Fw 187. It was obvious to the company that it would have to abandon development of the twin-engined Fw 187 and that development of the Jumo-engined Fw 187 was over for the time being.

All that Focke Wulf was left was the contract for the pre-production aircraft and the opportunity to gain experience in constructing high-performance combat aircraft. In the course of another meeting on future aircraft development programs for the *Luftwaffe* on 3 September 1939, even before the first flight of a pre-production Fw 187, the RLM took a position on the two-seat Fw 187: "...Fw 187 two-seat fighter with heavy armament and short range. Pre-production series under construction. No intention to introduce the type into service."

The comment "short range" is interesting, for the range of the Fw 187 was more than twice that of the Bf 109 or Bf 110. The administration casually terminated the fighter before it had a chance to demonstrate its performance capabilities. All of Focke Wulf's development work appeared to have been in vain.

The Bf 110 C began replacing the Bf 110 B in 1939. The C-version was the first to be equipped with the more powerful DB 601 engine. Here aircraft are seen on a front-line airfield.

In many photographs of Fw 190s under test, examples of the Fw 187 may be seen in the background. In this photograph, for example, two Fw 187s are visible in the background behind several Fw 190s. (Focke Wulf)

A Fw 187 A-0 banks away from the camera. Production was limited to five Zero-Series aircraft. (Focke Wulf)

The He 100 with Surface Evaporation Cooling

Despite the relatively low output of its Jumo 210 engines, the Fw 187 was able to demonstrate an impressive turn of speed. Focke Wulf had meanwhile become aware of the possibilities of surface evaporation cooling, as Heinkel had used this in its He 119 and He 100.

The He 100's coolant was pressurized and its temperature was approximately 110° Celsius. The liquid-cooled DB 601 A engine was capable of withstanding these temperatures. The coolant expanded to form steam. Steam from the centrifugal steam separator was deposited in cooling chambers which extended from the leading edge to the wing spar. These were made of copper-free aluminum alloy which was welded electrically. Later, parts of the fuselage were also used as cooling surfaces. The condensation was initially transferred by diaphragm pumps, later by injectors. Twenty-two small electric pumps returned the coolant to the engine. There was an indicator lamp in the cockpit of the He 100 for each of these pumps. The entire system proved to be quite troublesome. Although it was intended to dispense with a ventral radiator altogether, a retractable auxiliary radiator had to be installed for takeoffs.

Focke Wulf had plans to use this cooling principle for its Fw 187. In any case the Focke Wulf Fw 187 had much in common with the Heinkel He 100. Both aircraft were designed as high-speed fighters. Both designs emphasized maximum speed. Heinkel chose a single-engined solution, while Focke Wulf opted for two engines. A pre-production series of He 100s was built and, like the Fw 187, the aircraft were used for propaganda purposes. And finally, a number of He 100s were used by Heinkel in the industry defense role, as was the Fw 187.

Heinkel adopted surface evaporation cooling in an attempt to increase the maximum speed of the He 100.

The Fw 187 V5 Steam Hot Cooling

From very early in the Fw 187 program, Focke Wulf began considering the use of hot-cooled engines. At the time that the Fw 187 V1 was being developed, however, this was not possible with the Jumo 210. Tests found the Jumo 210 unsuitable for this type of cooling. Not until the advent of the DB 601 did it become a possibility. The principle can be described simply as follows: the coolant required by the engine is placed under pressure, allowing the engine to be operated at higher temperatures. A centrifugal steam separator is required to prevent vapor buildup.

It was not as simple as it seemed, however. While the existing literature attributes the Heinkel principle to the Fw 187, it was in fact an independent design. From the beginning, the Fw 187 V5 was earmarked for testing of the hot cooling system. The Fw 187 V6 is often mentioned in connection with "surface evaporation cooling". In fact, however, it was always the Fw 187 V5.

Focke Wulf began making extensive theoretical calculations for steam hot cooling as early as 1938. Working with Daimler Benz, Focke Wulf pursued development of the evaporation system and made it ready for production. Daimler Benz carried out an extensive test program to evaluate the new technology. Using an experimental system combining the second prototype of the DB 601 A engine and an evaporation system, Daimler Benz was able to successfully conclude the trials by July 1939. Using a so-called "swing stand", the experimental system was successfully tested in every flight attitude. The system could not simply be transferred to the Fw 187, however. Daimler Benz graphically described the development difficulties in Test Report No. 10 18 101 425:

1.) Development of the Evaporator

Focke Wulf developed an evaporation cooling system for its Fw 187, which we were supposed to test on the engine. We requested information on the evaporator and built a system based on our previous experience, taking into consideration the amount of space available.

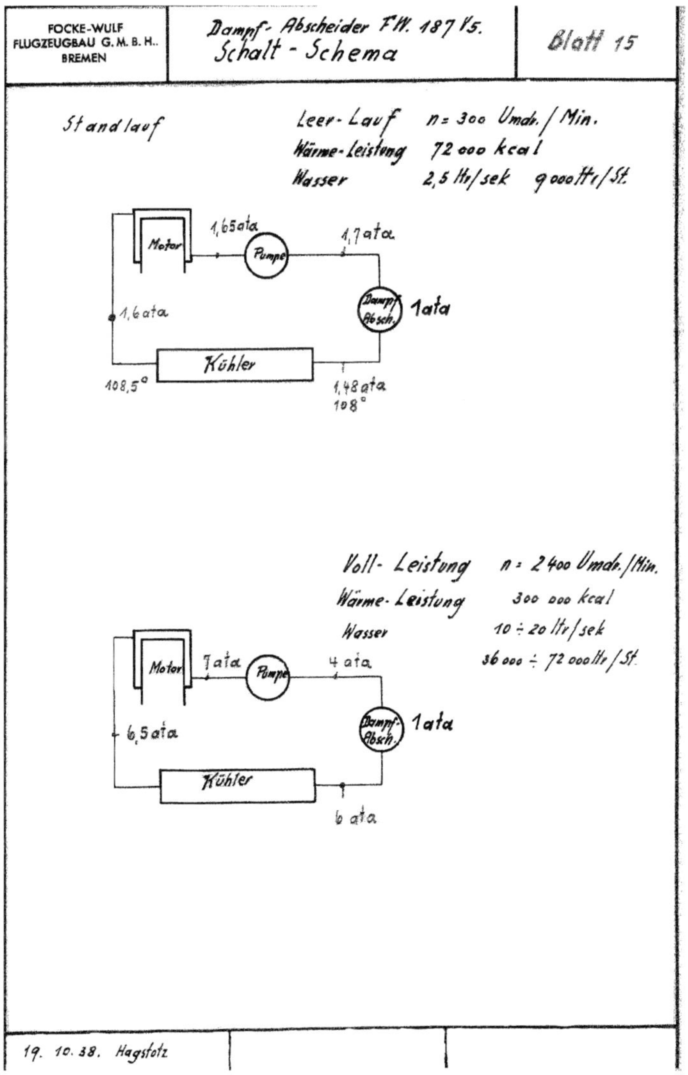

Original Focke Wulf drawing of the company's design for a hot-cooling system for the Fw 187.

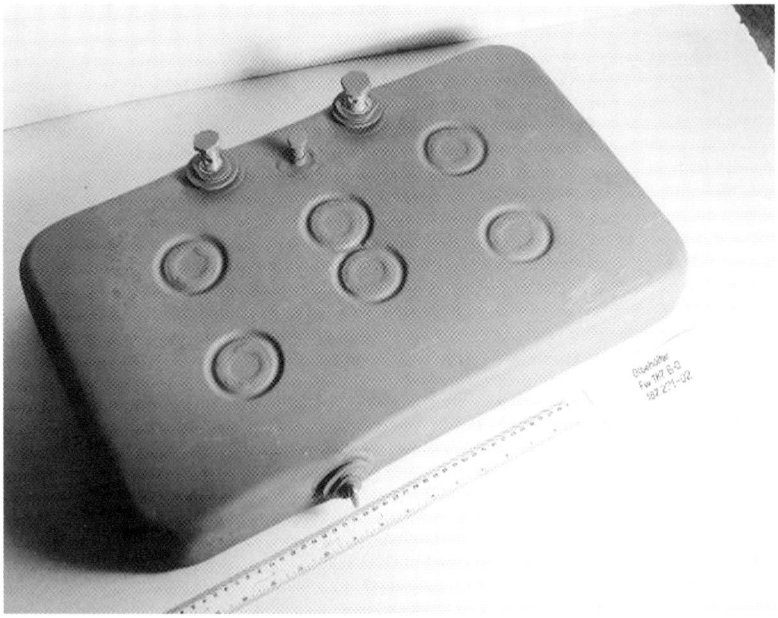

Even the Fw 187 B's oil tank appears small. (EADS Unternehmensarchiv Bremen)

The system proposed by us consisted of two vertically-arranged evaporators located at the cylinder coolant outlet and an additional water tank mounted forward around the gearbox. At the same time, Focke Wulf was engaged in developing its own system tailored precisely to their airframe. The system envisaged a horizontally-arranged evaporator behind the engine level with the water pump. Both arrangements also included two longitudinal coolers beneath the valve cover, which were to carry away up to 60% of the heat in the coolant.

As hot water evaporation tests without an engine were very difficult with regard to flow conditions, a switch was made to cold water. It was found that, with cold water, the efficiency of an evaporator could be determined by the clarity of the water leaving the system. A good evaporator removed all the foam present in the water, so that only foam-free water could be seen at the outlet. The installation of various windows in the evaporator allowed the flow of water to be studied precisely.

The Daimler Benz vertical evaporator was examined first. It turned out that neither the inlet nor outlet were in order. At the inlet our spring projected into the interior of the evaporator, thus disturbing the rotating water. As a result the entire film of water was very unsettled. An undisturbed flow of water into the evaporator was achieved by altering the shape of the nozzle and redesigning the spring.

The outlet from our evaporator was large, to allow all of the water to exit freely. This created a certain suction effect, which caused some of the removed foam to be carried along. These experiments showed that a certain level of water had to be maintained in the vertical evaporator. Any change created a gap which prevented the injector effect of the outflowing water. The width of the gap could be varied, and it was found that the most favorable width was 4 to 5 mm. Using cold water, that setting produced a foam-free exit from the evaporator.

Focke Wulf's evaporator is based on an entirely different principle. The evaporator is arranged horizontally and has two side inlets. There is an opening in the middle of the evaporator cylinder. The water passes through this opening into the secondary water tank and is returned to the water pump. The steam is carried away to the sides.

The characteristics of this evaporator were examined closely using cold water. It was found that Focke Wulf's evaporator, which had no nozzle spring, definitely required one, as this resulted in a much improved water flow. In the same way, the condensed water return could be located at a position in the evaporator which did not result in a disturbance of the water film.

In the horizontally arranged evaporator water flow is particularly important, in order to prevent suction effect by the outflowing water. Adjusting gap width to 4 mm results in covering of the gap. The water flowing in from the left and right meet at the gap, thickening the water film at that place and covering over the entire gap. As the water flowing out of the gap makes a twisting motion, an attempt was made to exploit this, using the kinetic energy of the water to create pressure before reaching the pump. A spiral volute was installed in place of the secondary water tank. This was aban-

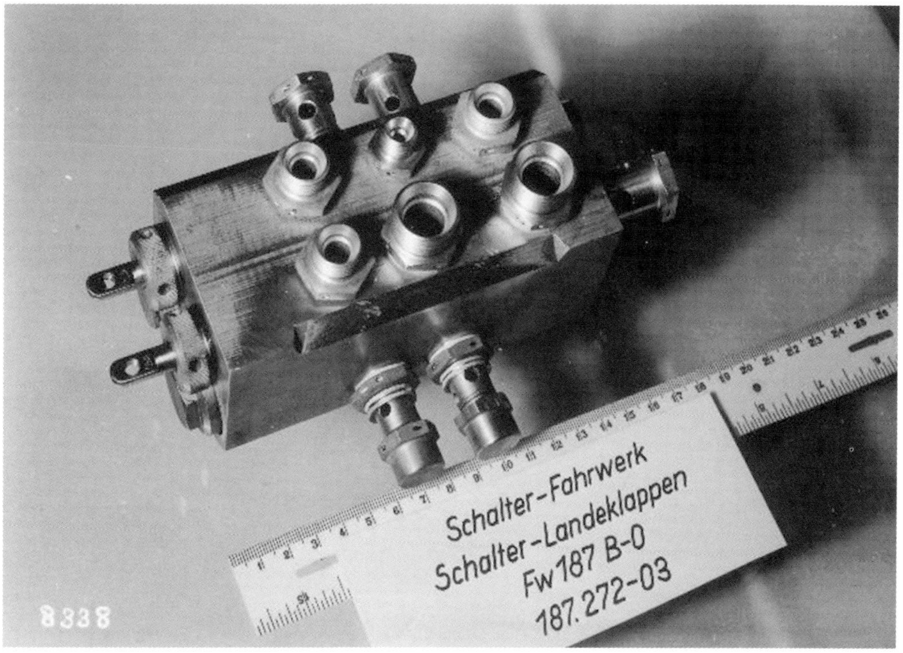

An example of the precision work done by the Focke Wulf Flugzeugbau. A combined switch for undercarriage and landing flaps. (EADS Unternehmensarchiv Bremen)

doned, however, because it proved impossible to eliminate foam from the outlet water. Various changes to the volute resulted in the ultimate version. As Focke Wulf had designed their system for a water volume of 45 liters, which was in constant circulation, an overflow had to be added to the horizontal evaporator so as to keep the steam outlet as dry as possible. This was achieved by installing a shutter while closely monitoring the thickness of the water film. All excess water flowed over the shutter into the secondary water tank. With this the cold water trials were terminated and the system was installed on the test bench with a DB 600 for the first time.

2.) Testing the System on the Test Bench

The system with a horizontally-arranged evaporator beneath the surface of the water was preferred. The illustration depicts the arrangement of this system. Initial trials revealed that the evaporator beneath the surface of the water worked very poorly. It constantly had to clear away the water lying above it, as a result of which the steam exited in spurts. As well, some of the steam reached the water pump, tearing the filaments. The system was subsequently modified to place the evaporator at the same level as our engine's ignition system. The evaporator, which was still exhibiting a number of shortcomings, was also redesigned. Furthermore, the two longitudinal coolers were installed. Condensed water return was achieved by a DBU pump. The revised system is illustrated in the accompanying sketch.

As shutting down the engine resulted in steam forming in the cylinder, a source of water was placed in front of the water pump. An intermediate tank with a capacity of 14 liters was installed, providing a water reserve should the engine suddenly start again. Favorable results were achieved with this arrangement.

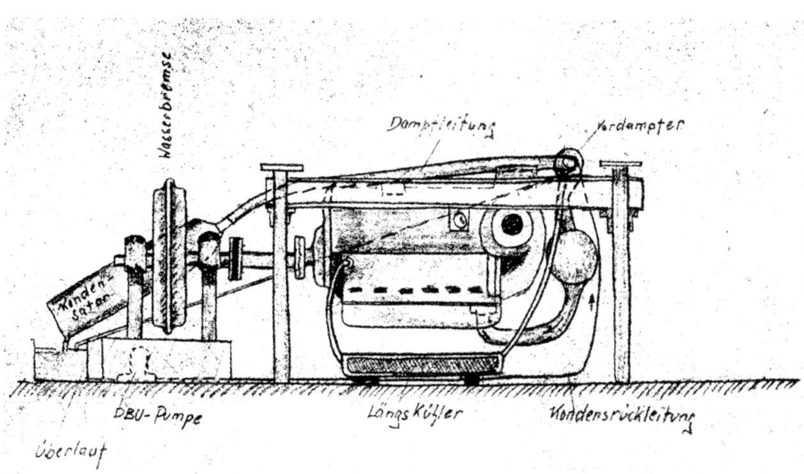

Compact technology behind the leading edge (removed). No space was wasted in the design of the Fw 187. (EADS Unternehmensarchiv Bremen)

The longitudinal coolers provided by Behr Zuffenhausen could not take the water pressure which built up and therefore had to be modified. The experiments were terminated as Focke Wulf was building an evaporator based on new findings. It was intended that the system would later be tested with a DB 601.

3.) Testing the System on the "Swing Stand"

After receiving the new evaporator, and the reinforced longitudinal coolers, the system was installed on the movable test stand. Much emphasis was placed on making the system as suitable as possible for use in aircraft.

Focke Wulf had planned to use a geared pump for condensation return, however this had to be replaced by an electrically-powered wing pump, as the former's flexible shaft kept breaking. The results with this system were satisfactory. Pressure increased slowly as engine speed increased, and it could be said that there was a certain amount of inertia.

The quantity of condensed and secondary water played a major role in the arrangement. It could be observed that the system performed better with the quantity of pumped-in water. The evaporator functioned poorly when the system was overfilled. The evaporation cooling worked flawlessly with approximately 16 liters of

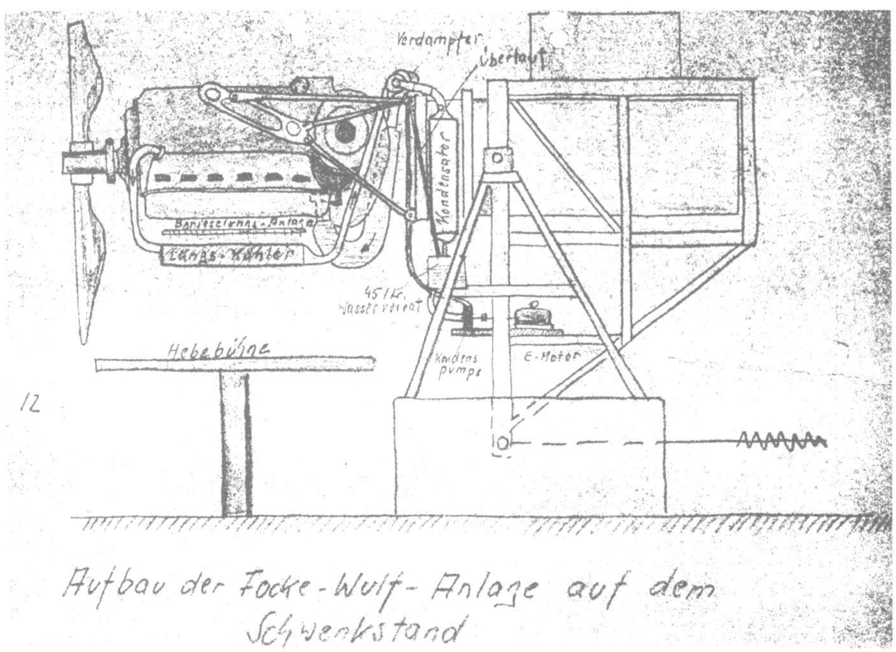

Drawing of the Focke Wulf system installed on the pivoting stand.

This Messerschmitt Bf 110 C, VB+TV, was used by Focke Wulf to test the hot-cooled DB 601 engine. (Focke Wulf)

condensed and secondary water. It is recommended, however, that this quantity be increased to 20 liters for safety reasons.

We tested the Focke Wulf evaporation cooling system in every possible flight attitude and no serious shortcomings were found. The tests were broken off when it was realized that there were no changes to the system which would result in improved performance. Focke Wulf installed this type of system in its Fw 187 airframe in order to conduct initial flight trials."

The system was installed in the Fw 187 V5 with minor modifications. The first live run by the system, on the port engine of the V5, took place on 15 September 1939. Unlike the test arrangement used by Daimler Benz, Focke Wulf placed the tank between the evaporator and the engine pump. The leader pipe was routed through the tank and its only connection with the contents of the tank was through several bore holes. As well, in contrast to the test arrangement, the condenser pump was dependent on engine rpm.

In the beginning it proved impossible to achieve a state of inertia with this system, instead the water was forced through the steam and overflow pipe into the wing. The system was modified and the steam tube was routed outside. A redesigned evaporator was also installed.

The first test run with the new evaporator took place on 19 September 1939. It was found that there was no water circulation in the right bank of cylinders at 1,400 rpm. At first, the return valve between the cylinder block and the water pump was thought to be the source of the problem. The system was then completely installed on the starboard engine, however the result was the same. A detailed analysis of the problem revealed the cross-section of the entry nozzle in front of the water pump was too large, resulting in too little pressure in front of the water pump. The nozzle cross-section was reduced and the engine-driven auxiliary water pump was replaced by one driven by an electric motor.

Several technical modifications were agreed upon to make the system more reliable for trials. For example, the auxiliary water pumps produced by Focke Wulf were to be sent to Daimler Benz in Untertürkheim. After testing of the entire pump assembly it was expected that Daimler Benz would return the modified components quickly. The V5's first flight took place in October 1939.

Until now the Fw 187 V5, CI+NY, has usually been identified as a Fw 187 A-0 pre-production aircraft powered by Jumo 210 engines. As may be seen, this was not the case, for the Fw 187 V5 was designed from the beginning for DB 601 engines and evaporation cooling. For trials with the evaporation cooling system, the V5 was equipped with two of the scarce DB 601 prototype engines, specifically the DB 601 V40 and V42. These two engines were based on the 1,100 h.p. DB 601 A. Daimler Benz was convinced that the new cooling system was the way of the future, and subsequently proposed a series of new DB 601 variants, the H to the M, with hot steam cooling. The variants differed mainly in having different re-

From the beginning, the compact DB 601 was the engine desired by Focke Wulf for the Fw 187. The engine was a development of the DB 600 and was almost twice as powerful as the Jumo 210. (DaimlerChrysler Archive)

duction gearing. These DB 601 engines were capable of producing 1,350 h.p. for one minute at ground level.

Initial flight trials with the Fw 187 V5 revealed a maximum speed of 635 km/h at low level. The V5's performance made a good impression on the RLM. Interest in the Fw 187 was reawakened.

Focke Wulf continued calibration flights with the Fw 187 V5 into 1941, an indication that the new cooling system had not been abandoned and was still under development. Testing of the Fw 187 V5 was finally concluded in February 1942. Focke Wulf recorded: "Fw 187 V5 grounded – testing of the evaporation cooling system terminated."

The Fw 187 B

On 4 March 1938 Focke Wulf received instructions to begin design work on a version of the Fw 187 powered by Daimler Benz DB 601 engines and to construct a mock-up. Focke Wulf once again set to work. With the more powerful DB 601 engines, the Fw 187 would, for the first time, have a chance to show what a brilliant design it was. On 14 September 1939, after the successful conclusion of preliminary work, Focke Wulf received a contract from the RLM to redesign the Fw 187 to accept the new Daimler Benz DB 601 engine. Soon afterwards, Focke Wulf received contracts to construct the Fw 187 V5 (*Werknummer* 1976) and three Fw 187 B-0 pre-production machines (*Werknummer* 1977, 1978 and 1979). The V5 was thus the prototype of the Fw 187 B-series. By the summer of 1939 work on the V5 was 82% complete and it was still expected that construction would be completed in July. At that time the first pre-production aircraft was already 75% complete and the other two machines 60%. In addition to the Fw 187 B-0s under construction, Focke Wulf documents were already making reference to a Fw 187 B-1.

The second machine under construction, *Werknummer* 1977, was later redesignated the Fw 187 V7. This aircraft was supposed to undertake a number of official record attempts. Focke Wulf's goal, to surpass the Me 209's speed record, was an ambitious one. The Me 209 had established the record of 755 km/h on 26 April 1939. For its attempt on the record, the Fw 187 V7 was to be powered by specially boosted DB 601 engines. But time was working against Focke Wulf. On 12 September 1939, shortly after the out-

Testing the exhaust system of the Fw 187 V7. (Creek)

Sensational photographs of the Fw 187 V7, published here for the first time. The photos also give some indication of the effort expended in exhaust gas mixture experiments on the Fw 187 V7. They also prove that the outer wings were removed for these experiments. This was an ignominious end for the Fw 187 V7, which had been intended for an attempt on the Me 209's world speed record. (Creek)

break of war, work on the Fw 187 V7 was officially halted. The aircraft was complete, with the exception of the special DB 601 engines. The V7 was never completed and Focke Wulf later used it for experiments in parallel with the Fw 187 V5. Like the Fw 187 V5, experiments with the V7 were halted in February 1942 and the aircraft was placed in storage. Although Focke Wulf produced a Specification of the highly interesting B-series, it and many other documents from that period remain missing.

Like the Fw 187 A, development of the higher-performance B-series was also suspended. The exact reason for this is not known. It is possible, however, that the RLM viewed the type as not yet fully developed or too prone to technical problems, like the He 100. On the other hand, the Fw 187 B may have fallen victim to the rationalization of aircraft types for the *Luftwaffe* which resulted from the outbreak of the Second World War.

Opposite: Installation of the new DB 601 engine in the Fw 187 V5. Note the longitudinal radiator under the engine block. In the background is Bf 110 C, VB+TV, which was used by Focke Wulf as a test bed.

This photograph depicts the installation of the DB 601 V39 complete with motor mounts in the airframe of the Fw 187 V7.

Impressive views of the Fw 187 V5. The aircraft is parked on a wet concrete apron in front of the huge hangar doors of the Bremen factory. Note the streamlined radiator intakes in the front view.

Daimler Benz DB 601 H	1 350 PS	VH = 4,8 km	1939

Bauart: 12-Zylinder Einspritz-Flugmotor, flüssigkeitgekühlt
Bauform: Reihenmotor in 60° V-Form mit hängenden Zylindern

Arbeitsverfahren: 4-Takt, Höhenlader, (sog. Dampfheißkühlung)

Bohrung:	150	mm	
Hub:	160	mm	
Hub/Bohrung:	1,067		
Zylinderhubraum:	2,83	l	
Gesamthubraum	33,9	l	
Verdichtungsgrad:	1:7,2		
Länge des Triebwerkes:	2 303	mm	
Höhe des Triebwerkes:	1 035	mm	
Breite des Triebwerkes:	739	mm	
Gewicht des Triebwerkes (Trockengewicht):	660	kg	
Einbaugewicht des Triebwerkes (mit Zusatzgeräten):	790	kg	
Höchstleistung bei 2 700 U/min in 0 m Höhe:	1 350	PS	(1')
Höchstleistung bei 2 700 U/min in 4 800 m Höhe:	1 320	PS	(1')
Kurzleistung bei 2 500 U/min in 0 m Höhe:	1 200	PS	(5')
Kurzleistung bei 2 500 U/min in 4 900 m Höhe:	1 200	PS	(5')
Dauerleistung bei 2 300 U/min in 0 m Höhe:	1 000	PS	(30')
Dauerleistung bei 2 300 U/min in 5 100 m Höhe:	1 040	PS	
Volldruckhöhe:	4 800	m	
Zylinderleistung:	112,50	PS	
Hubraumleistung:	39,82	PS/l	
Leistungsgewicht:	0,48	kg/PS	
Hubraumgewicht:	19,48	kg/l	
Kraftstoffverbrauch bei Kurzleistung:	215	g/PS h	
Kraftstoffverbrauch bei Dauerleistung:	205	g/PS h	
Schmierstoffverbrauch:	4-8	g/PS h	

Einlaßventile/Zylinder: 2
gesteuert durch: Königswelle mit gemeinsamen Nocken für Ein- und Auslaß
Auslaßventile/Zylinder: 2
gesteuert durch: Königswelle mit gemeinsamen Nocken für Ein- und Auslaß

Luftschrauben-Untersetzungsgetriebe:	1:1,685
Drehrichtung Kurbelwelle:	links
Drehrichtung Luftschraube:	rechts

Anlasser:	Bosch AL-SGC 24 DR 2 Schwungkraftanlasser von Hand od. elektrisch
Zündanlage:	1 Bosch ZM 12 CR 8 Zwillingsmagnet
Kühlwasserumlauf:	Daimler Benz Kreiselpumpe
Gemischbildung durch:	1 Bosch PZ 12 HP 110/14 Einspritzpumpe für 12 Zylinder
Schmierung:	Daimler Benz Druck-Schmierstoffpumpe (Zahnradpumpe)

Bemerkungen: zwei Bosch DW 250 ET 7 Zündkerzen je Zylinder
Zündfolge: 1-8-5-10-3-7-6-11-2-9-4-12-1
Kraftstoffpumpe: Graetzin ZD 500 E Doppelpumpe

Lader: einstufiges Daimler Benz Schleudergebläse mit automatischem Antrieb über eine hydraulisch schaltbare Kupplüng mit barometrischer Regelung.

Der DB 601 H Flugmotor entsprach in seinen Leistungen und dem konstruktiven Aufbau dem DB 600 E Motor. Um mit kleineren Wasserkühlern auszukommen, wurde bei dem DB 601 H Motor die sog. Dampfheißkühlung angewendet, d.h. das Kühlwasser wurde unter Druck gesetzt, um das Triebwerk mit höheren Temperaturen fahren zu können. Das Triebwerk DB 601 H erhielt deshalb zusätzlich einen Zentrifugal-Dampfabscheider, um Dampfblasen im Kühlwasserumlauf zu vermeiden.

Daimler Benz DB 601 H specification sheet. This engine was one of a whole series of hot-cooled power plants.

The Fw 187 in the Industry Defense Role

The *Luftwaffe* expected Allied air raids on military targets in Germany as early as 1940. These targets included aircraft manufacturers. Located near the north coast in Bremen, Focke Wulf was especially threatened. To better protect the Bremen Flugzeugwerk against Allied air attacks, Focke Wulf had to establish a capable industry defense system. This included a Factory Defense Squadron, which was to defend Bremen and Hamburg-Wenzendorf. The important question of pilots for the *6. Werksschutzstaffel*, as the unit was officially designated, answered itself. They took the pilots who were there, test and acceptance pilots. The factory defense pilots included Hans Sander, Kurt Mehlhorn, August Linde, Ewald Rohlfs, Walter Schorn, Hans Schubert, Ludwig Vogel, Uffz. Helmuth Bischoff, Gefr. Hermann Schlegel and *Flugkapitän* Wolfgang Stein (head of the acceptance pilots), plus Kurt Tank himself. In the process Kurt Tank was promoted to the rank of *Hauptmann*. In response to the establishment order, on 13 February 1940 Focke Wulf reported to the RLM that the unit had four serviceable Fw 187s. The Focke Wulf test pilots flew the first industry defense missions in the period from 4 April to 23 August 1940.

The company pilots conducted numerous test flights with the four available Fw 187s. Focke Wulf now designated the machines Fw 187 S. Emphasis was placed on the cold-start procedure and testing the aircraft's radio equipment. By mixing fuel with the engine oil, it was possible to take off without first warming up the engines. It was important to determine how much fuel had to be added. The radio system proved extremely troublesome. In some cases transmission range was only three kilometers, whereas the requirement was sixty kilometers. Improvements were made to the system and the desired range was eventually achieved.

The test pilots were visibly aware of what might lie ahead of them. Hans Sander remarked of the test flights that he had to lower his seat to the maximum to be able to see all of the aiming circle of the reflector gunsight. As a result, the installation had to be modified. A number of minor problems were found and corrected, for example the tailwheel extension mechanism, too much play in the elevator and the canopy locking system. During this hectic test phase both Hans Sander and Kurt Mehlhorn flew the Fw 187 S2, S4 and S5 (*Werknummer* 1968, 1974 and 1975). These three Fw 187 A-0

The radio operator climbs into the cockpit of a Fw 187. Note the bulged machine-gun fairings and the canopy-opening mechanism. (Focke Wulf)

Another perspective: the crew of a Fw 187 exiting the cockpit. (Petrick)

Line-up of three aircraft of the Factory Protection Staffel in Bremen. (Focke Wulf)

Staged photo of air and ground crew running to aircraft "Yellow 4" in preparation for a scramble. (Focke Wulf)

pre-production aircraft were assigned to the factory defense flight, along with the Fw 187 V5. In Tank's log book, however, CI+NY appears as CI+NX. On 8 May 1940 these aircraft were joined by the Fw 187 S3, *Werknummer* 1969, which served as the unit's reserve aircraft.

Hans Sander's combat preparation flights took place in the period from 16 March to 8 April 1940. As a rule they were flown with just the pilot on board. Ballast had to be placed in the rear seat to allow three-point landings to be made. In this configuration, take-off weight fully equipped was just 4850 kg.

There are many photographs showing the three Fw 187 A-0s wearing tactical numbers. Like the series of propaganda photographs depicting the single-engine He 100 D-0, they were intended to convince the enemy that Germany had a new twin-engined fighter in service.

Ground personnel moving a Fw 187 A-0. This series of photographs was intended to document the unit's operational readiness. No spurious unit emblems were applied to the Fw 187s, as was the case in propaganda photographs of the He 100. Also unlike the He 100, the Fw 187 was flown on operational missions. (Focke Wulf)

Yellow 7 and Yellow 1 are readied for a sortie. Hauptmann Kurt Tank flew several industry defense missions in both aircraft. (Focke Wulf)

The crew of Yellow 4 boards their aircraft in preparation for a scramble. Note the opening mechanism of the forward canopy section and the extended boarding ladder. Just visible on the fuselage is the overpainted manufacturer's code CA+WZ. (Petrick)

During its brief existence, the Industry Defense Squadron was incorporated into the fighter unit JG 1. According to Hans Sander, it flew as part of Johannes Steinhoff's *Staffel*. Hans Sander flew his first industry defense mission on 5 May 1940, in the aircraft bearing the tactical number "7". The aircraft flew defensive patrols as well as flak familiarization and practice flights. In the period from 21 June to 9 July 1940, Tank flew live missions in CI+NX, "1"and "7".

Tank also made flights to Jever and Marx, where *Luftwaffe* interceptor units were based. Tank often remained there for several days, and it is quite likely that the *Luftwaffe* units were given an opportunity to familiarize themselves with the Fw 187. It is a fact that the *Geschwaderstab* of JG 1 was based at Jever at that time.

According to Hans Sander, missions during the first industry defense period were hampered by the dispersement of personnel. As well, crews lacked sufficient experience with the cold-start procedure. Attrition took its toll on the few Fw 187 A-0s. First *Werknummer* 1974 made a crash-landing on 16 May 1940. The aircraft's damaged engines were removed and sent to Junkers. It was not until 26 June that two replacements were installed and the aircraft returned to service. Soon afterwards, on 2 July, 1975, undercarriage trouble resulted in a forced landing. The aircraft was heavily damaged and later had to be scrapped.

It is difficult to say how successful these missions really were. Focke Wulf company pilot *Flugkapitän* Wolfgang Stein was awarded the Iron Cross, Second Class for his missions in the Fw 187. In May 1943 Stein shot down a Spitfire. It was also claimed that test pilot Kurt Mehlhorn, who crashed to his death during an industry defense mission two years later, also achieved success flying the Fw 187, however the only proof of this is contained in his obituary in the Focke Wulf company newspaper "*Der Condor*", which stated that he... "shot down several enemy aircraft in just a few missions".

Flugkapitän Wolfgang Stein (far right) seen with Focke Wulf engineer Rietz (top right) and Kurt Bühlingen of III./JG 2 in Cherbourg. Stein was awarded the Iron Cross, Second Class for successful operations in the Fw 187.

Kurt Tank is Chased by Bf 109 Fighters

The following account is from the book *Nerves, Heart and Slide Rule* by Heinz Conradis:

It was not long after the outbreak of the war, and English reconnaissance aircraft and light bombers had already made brief visits to the German Baltic Coast. The Fw 187, one of a handful of types completely unknown to friend or foe, was to take part in gunnery exercises near Wangerooge. The large wooden targets were already in place. Tank was flying the aircraft himself, for the debate as to whether or not this twin-engined design would be built now that the war was raging was still going on. A local Bf 109 from Wangerooge airfield had been assigned as a guide and comparison aircraft, and both now took turns diving at the target, firing, and pulling up.

There were no radio communications and neither pilot was aware that British twin-engined bombers were approaching. A *Staffel* of Bf 109s had been scrambled and they were now patrolling along the islands searching for prey. They were eager for action, for to date they had had little contact with enemy aircraft. Over Wangerooge they sighted a twin-engined aircraft with a Bf 109 behind it. Then red muzzle flashes from the Messerschmitt's cannon. It was one of theirs! After him!

In a flash, like a swarm of hornets, the *Staffel* was behind the Englishman, who, after all, already had a German fighter on his tail.

Tank noticed nothing. He only knew that there was a Bf 109 in front of him and was unaware that others were lining up in firing position behind him. Thos on the Wangerooge airfield below held their breath. O. Behrens, the technical officer and test director of *Jagdgeschwader 1*, who later became very close to Tank, was certain that he had no chance. But then, just in time, the leader of the German fighters saw the black crosses and did not fire. Tank saw the fighters as they broke away and landed as quickly as he could.

Early in the war Kurt Tank received an unpleasant surprise while flying the Fw 187, when he was almost attacked by a Staffel of Messerschmitt Bf 109s. Here Prof. Tank is seen climbing into the cockpit of a Fw 187.

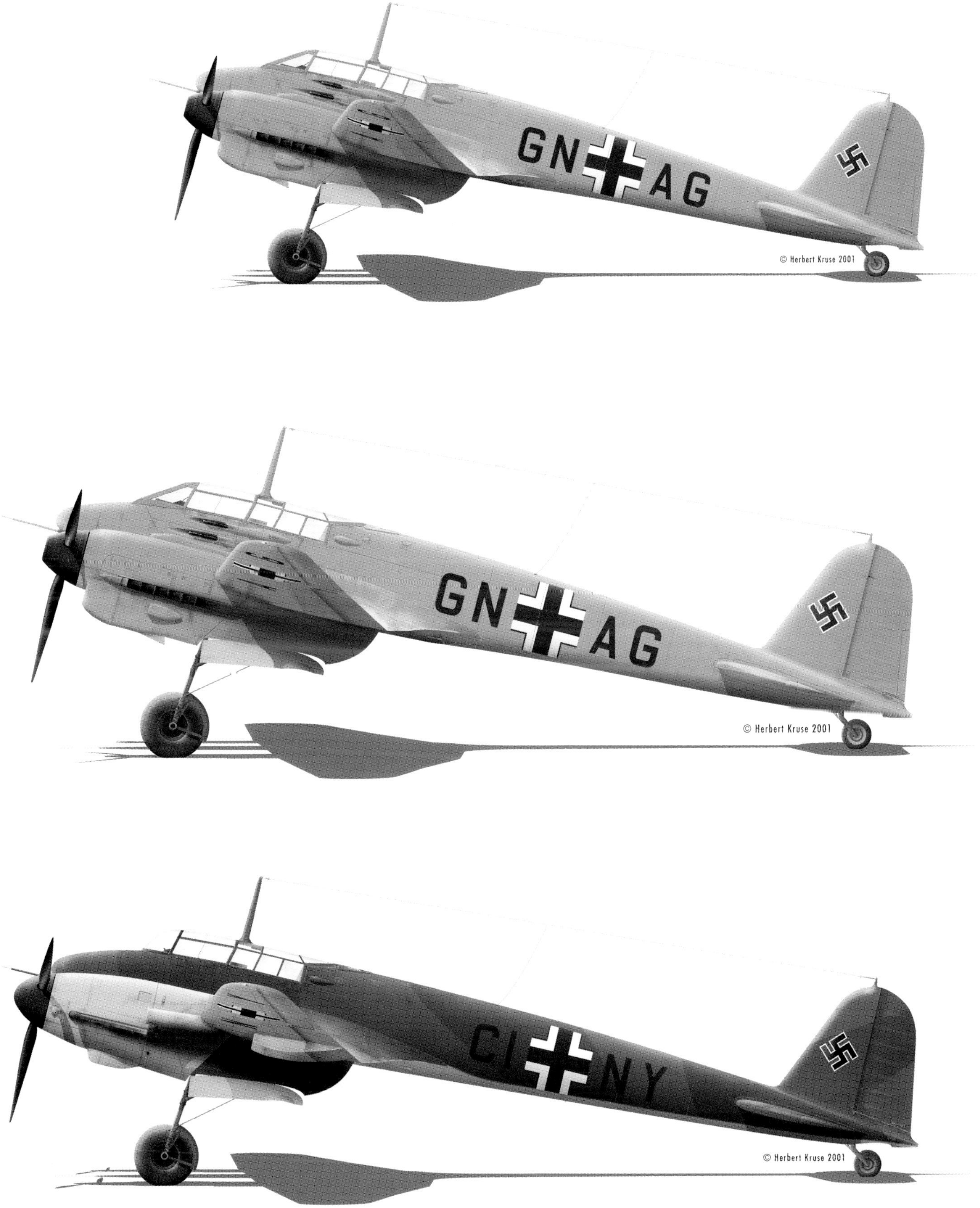

Side views of the Focke Wulf Fw 187.

The Battle of Britain Changes Nothing

In the initial stages of the war the *Zerstörer* philosophy gained credence in the *Luftwaffe*. An early high point was the engagement over the Helgoland Bight on 17 December 1939. Early detection of a formation of 22 Wellington bombers allowed 32 Bf 109s and 16 Bf 110s to intercept the enemy bombers over the North Sea. Twelve British bombers were shot down, of which nine were credited to the Bf 110s of I./ZG 76.

At the start of the Battle of Britain in August 1940, the *Luftwaffe* was able to muster 230 Bf 110s. By then the *Zerstörer* units were equipped with the improved Bf 110 C and D. As the Bf 109 suffered from limited range, it was intended that the Bf 110s should provide long-range escort for German bomber formations. This was in fact the role of the *Zerstörer*. As the few encounters over France had shown, the Bf 110 was no match for the faster and more maneuverable Hurricanes and Spitfires of the Royal Air Force. In the Battle of Britain the Bf 110's lack of maneuverability, which had been reported earlier by the *E-Stelle Rechlin*, became apparent for all to see. The direct result was heavy losses, and the *Zerstörer* units had to be withdrawn from the fighting. By 28 September 1940 the number of serviceable Bf 110s had fallen to just 100, and production could not keep pace with losses. The Bf 110 had proved a complete failure over England in its intended role of strategic fighter. One of the factors which contributed to this failure was a lack of flexibility on the part of *Luftwaffe* planners. As early as the fighting in Poland, Bf 110 pilots knew that the Bf 110 lacked maneuverability. As a result, they adopted the so-called "climb and dive tactic", which proved very effective. This tactic saw the Messerschmitts climb above enemy formations and attack in a shallow dive. In the Battle of Britain the *Zerstörer* units were forced to abandon this tactic with devastating consequences. What the *Luftwaffe* lacked was an effective long-range escort fighter like the Fw 187, with speed and maneuverability equal to that of single-engined fighters. This was exactly the role for which Prof. Tank had designed the Fw 187. In fairness, however, it must be said that subsequent versions of the Bf 110 achieved success in the fighter-bomber role. The Bf 110 C-4/B fighter-bomber was powered by more powerful DB 601 N engines and was capable of carrying 500 kg of bombs.

Yellow 7, a Fw 187 A-0 pre-production aircraft, banks toward the camera. (Focke Wulf)

The *Luftwaffe* high command was aware of these facts, nevertheless it failed to draw any decisive conclusions from them. There were several reasons for this. For one, it would have amounted to an admission that the RLM's decision to adopt the *Zerstörer* class of aircraft had been wrong. As well, there was no time to refight the Battle of Britain, as military events were proceeding apace. The *Luftwaffe* stuck with the Bf 110, even though a superior alternative was available, namely the Fw 187.

Interlude in Denmark and the Vaerløse Aerial Gunnery School

At the end of August 1940 Focke Wulf's industry defense missions were officially called to a halt. Although the subsequent fate of all of the Fw 187 A-0 pre-production aircraft is uncertain, it is known that a number of aircraft were sent to the *Zerstörer* Replacement Training *Gruppe* in Vaerløse, Denmark.

One of the pilots who flew the Fw 187 A-0 at with 2. Staffel of the *Zerstörer* Replacement Training *Gruppe* in Vaerløse was Lt. Fritz Carstens. After his training there he joined III./NJG 1 as a night fighter pilot. He later served as *Staffelkapitän* in III./NJG 4 and ended the war with III./NJG 5, also as a *Staffelkapitän*. He described his experiences flying the Fw 187 A-0 in Vaerløse:

"After completing my *Zerstörer* training in Schleissheim, I was assigned to the 2. Staffel of the *Zerstörer* Replacement Training *Gruppe* in Vaerløse from 1 September to 10 October 1940 prior to joining the night fighters. In that time I flew the Fw 187 three or four times. I first made a brief test flight unaccompanied. Then I was ordered to intercept an unidentified object at high altitude, which could be seen as a light in a clear blue sky. I climbed to 8700 meters, the highest altitude I had reached so far, and determined that the object was still far away and that its position was not changing. In my opinion it could only have been a star visible in daylight. As the Fw 187 was beginning to become "sloppy" and the engines could

Fw 187 A-0, CA+WZ, is refueled and readied for the next sortie in Vaerløse, Denmark. (Udo Trimper)

The two competing designs side by side. Parked next to Bf 110 B, BV+EX, is Fw 187 A, GN+AG. In May 1943 both machines were on strength with the Vaerløse Aerial Gunnery School. (Meyer)

Operational photographs of Fw 187 *Zerstörer* are rare. Depicted here is NJ+CA, which cannot be directly linked to Vaerløse. NJ+CA was destroyed in April 1942 when it stalled and crashed while on approach to land.

These photographs show a Fw 187 A-0 (left) and a Bf 110 during air firing in Vaerløse. The Fw 187's pilot was obviously an excellent shot, for the target is obscured by fountains of sand from the impacting rounds. Behind the dunes is the Baltic Sea. (Carstens)

Lt. Fritz Carstens in Laon, France in 1944...

...and his radio operator Fw. Herbert Meyer. Note the "squiggle" camouflage pattern on their Bf 110.

not provide the power to continue climbing, I broke off the flight and landed.

On another occasion I flew a practice sortie with a Messerschmitt Bf 110. I found that I could easily outmaneuver the Bf 110 in a turn. Later in the war I flew the Bf 110 G and Ju 88 G night fighters. The Fw 187 was by far the most maneuverable aircraft that I flew during training or later in service with the night fighters. Not only was it much more maneuverable than the Bf 110, it also climbed better. The Fw 187 caused absolutely no problems on takeoff or landing."

This example shows that the available Fw 187 A-0s were used in an operational role as well as for training. The author was fortunate to locate a pilot like Herr Carstens, who had actually flown the Fw 187.

In April 1941 NJ+CA was involved in a crash. The aircraft stalled while on approach to land and came down in a wood. The Fw 187 was completely destroyed, however the pilot survived with serious injuries. Although it is thought that this aircraft was *Werknummer* 1969, there is no conclusive proof.

In any case, only two Fw 187 A-0s remained on strength with the aerial gunnery school in Vaerløse from the end of October 1941 to August 1942, namely *Werknummer* 1968 and 1974. CA+WZ was flown by Uffz. Hans Müller on 1 July. The aircraft was also flown that day by Oblt. Kurt Ventzke, who also flew GN+AG on 8 July. During that same period *Oberleutnant* H. Heisel flew the Fw 187 with the factory code GN+AG on 7 July and CA+WZ on 15 August 1942. Oberleutnant Heisel was a member of ZG 26 "*Horst Wessel*".

At Vaerløse the unit removed all the weapons from *Werknummer* 1968 (four MG 17 and two MG FF) and replaced them with an experimental installation of a single MK 101 cannon with an installed weight of 185.5 kg. The conversion was completed in April-May 1942 and from then on the aircraft must have flown operationally with the Mk 101. To date no firing results for the Fw 187 armed with the MK 101 have been found.

A beautiful photograph in spite of its poor quality. A Fw 187 A-0 flies low over an area of lakes.

Two photographs of CA+WZ in Vaerløse. The aircraft's lengthy service life there speaks for the quality of the Fw 187.

The streamlined form of the Bf 110 B in flight. Pilots complained about the type's poor maneuverability. (EADS Unternehmensarchiv Ottobrunn via Ebert)

Beginning in 1941 live missions were flown against enemy incursions. On 29 August 1943 aircraft from Vaerløse, including one Fw 187, were scrambled to intercept English intruders.

It has been claimed that for a brief period in the winter of 1940-41 at least three Fw 187 A-0s were assigned to the *Zerstörerstaffel* (*13. Staffel*) of JG 77 in Norway. No proof of this has been discovered, however it is unlikely that the aircraft saw any action with JG 77.

The Fw 187 was much more maneuverable than the Bf 110. In the air the Bf 110 resembled a bomber, whereas the Fw 187 had the appearance of a fighter aircraft.

The Fw 187 as a Twin-Engined Dive Bomber

By mid-1940 it had become clear to Focke Wulf that neither the Fw 187 A or the more powerful Fw 187 B were going to enter production. Focke Wulf subsequently tried to modify the Fw 187 for the dive bombing role. Two new Specifications were issued. Specification No. 233 was for a twin-engined, single-seat dive bomber and No. 235 for a twin-engined, two-seat dive bomber.

The single-seat version was to be powered by two Daimler Benz DB 601 F engines each producing 1,350 h.p. for takeoff. Wingspan was 15 meters, length 12.15 meters and wing area 36 square meters. The fuselage was to be an all-metal stressed-skin structure. Armament was to consist of four MG 17 machine-guns and two MG 151 cannon. Two MG 17s were to be installed in the fuselage nose, with the remaining guns beneath the pilot's seat. Standard bomb load was 500 kg. Nominal takeoff weight was 7500 kg. Maximum bomb load in overloaded condition was 2000 kg. Three bomb racks were provided, one beneath the fuselage and one under each wing between the fuselage and engine nacelle. The bomb rack for the fuselage store was recessed. The fuselage store could be released in a vertical dive without use of the automatic pull-out mechanism. The wing stores could only be released in a vertical dive with the use of the automatic pull-out mechanism. Without the automatic pull-out mechanism the wing stores were limited to dive angles of 60 degrees or less. Planned radio equipment consisted of a FuG XVII and FuG XXV.

To date no drawing of the single-seat dive bomber variant has been discovered. A drawing of the two-seat dive bomber contained in Specification No. 235 has survived, however. It shows a twin-engined machine with BMW 801 engines. Although no performance figures are given, the drawing does illustrate the weapons installation.

Specification for the Single-Engine Dive Bomber Design

Wingspan		15 m
Length		12.15 m
Height		5.36 m
Wing area		36 m2
Armament		4 x MG 17 with 1,200 rounds per gun
		2 x MG 151 with 600 rounds per gun
Equipped weight		5440 kg
Crew 1 man		90 kg
Ammunition		382 kg
Fuel		1000 kg
Oil		80 kg
Bombs		500 kg
Gross weight		7500 kg
Maximum speed at low level		480 km/h
	at 2100 m	530 km/h
	at 4000 m	567 km/h
	at 6000 m (max. boost altitude)	605 km/h
	at 8000 m	590 km/h
Range with 500 kg fuselage store		1350 km
Range with 1000 kg of stores on wing racks and 1000 kg fuel tank beneath fuselage		2600 km (overload)
Service ceiling	10000 m	
Time to climb at 7500 kg	to 1000 m	1.4 min.
	to 2000 m	2.8 min.
	to 4000 m	5.7 min.
	to 6000 m	8.9 min.
	to 8000 m	14.2 min.

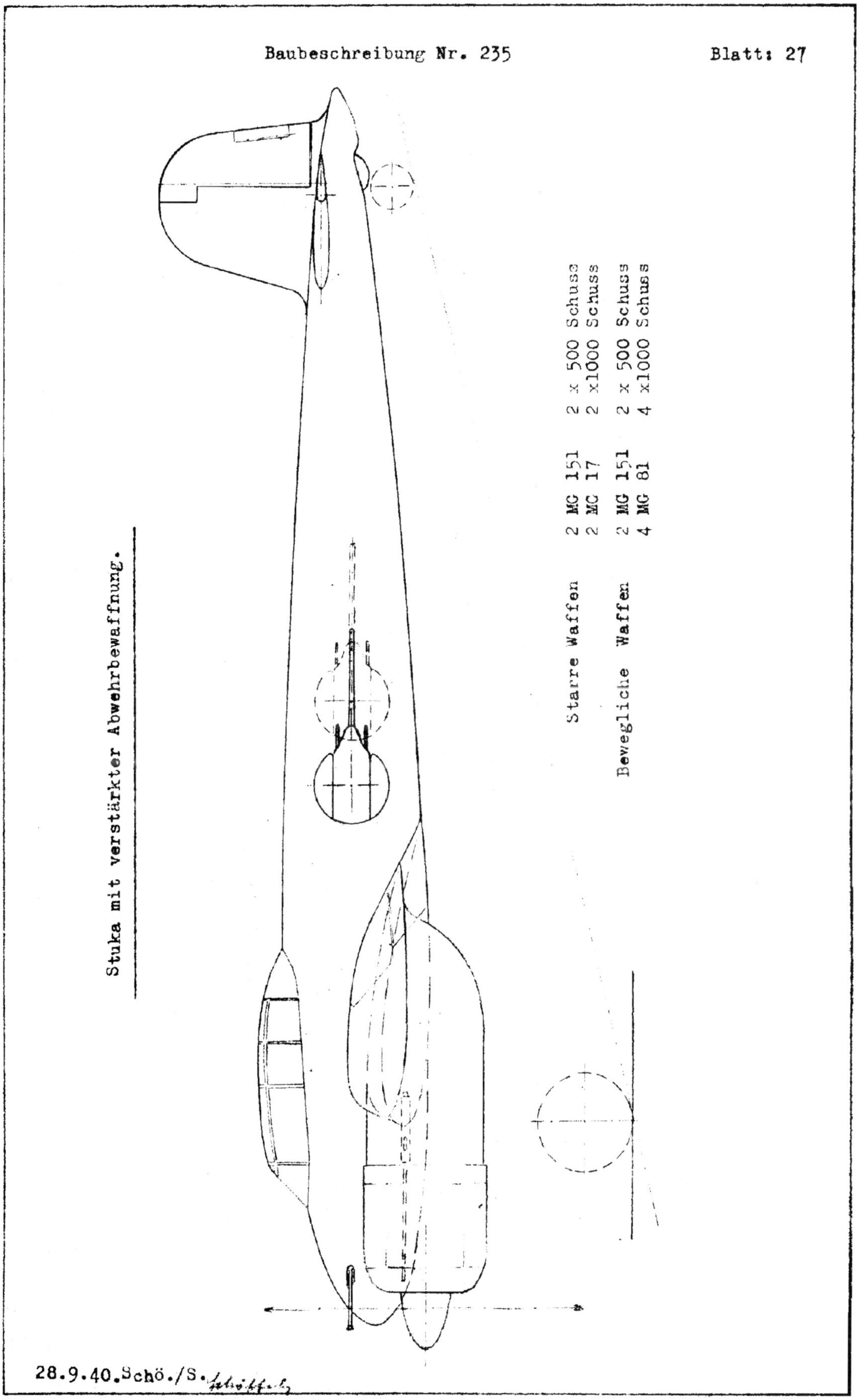

Baubeschreibung Nr. 235
Blatt: 27
Stuka mit verstärkter Abwehrbewaffnung.
Starre Waffen 2 MG 151 2 x 500 Schuss
2 MG 17 2 x1000 Schuss
Bewegliche Waffen 2 MG 151 2 x 500 Schuss
4 MG 81 4 x1000 Schuss
28.9.40.Schö./S.

The Messerschmitt Bf 110 in the Night Fighter Role

As the weight of German bombing raids increased, English resistance grew ever more determined. The RAF launched the first tentative raids on German targets while the Battle of Britain was still raging. The Handley Page Hampden, Vickers Wellington and Armstrong Whitworth Whitley were all first-generation bombers. Like the contemporary German bombers, they had a modest defensive armament and were underpowered. Over the next two years they were replaced by more powerful four-engined types, the Short Stirling, Handley Page Halifax and Avro Lancaster. These four-engined machines were capable of penetrating deep into Germany with heavy bomb loads and were faster and more heavily armed than their predecessors.

The start of the British bombing campaign resulted in the formation of an improvised German night fighter force. The first night fighters were converted Messerschmitt Bf 110 C heavy fighters. The performance of these early night fighters was poor, however this was not a serious handicap in the beginning. The Bf 110 was not equipped with airborne radar, as no such equipment existed in Germany at that time. Consequently the first *Gruppe* of NJG 1, which was formed at Venlo, Holland, had to depend on searchlights to locate enemy aircraft. Once spotted, enemy aircraft were attacked visually.

Successes were modest, and there were increasing calls from the night fighter pilots for airborne radar to enable them to locate

In 1943 the Bf 110 was still carrying the main load in the night defense of Germany. The Messerschmitt fighter had to remain in service as no suitable replacement could be found. Replacement by the He 219, for example, was out of the question. (Carstens)

The Messerschmitt Bf 110 C was used in the formative period of the German night fighter arm in 1940. These aircraft had neither airborne radar nor flame dampers. Seen here are two black-painted Bf 110 night fighters of NJG 1 in 1941. The night fighter emblem is clearly visible on the fuselage nose. (Carstens)

enemy aircraft on their own. The first German air interception radar was the FuG 202 by Telefunken. In 1943 the standard German night fighter was the Bf 110 F-4, which was powered by two Daimler Benz DB 601 F engines. The external antennas, 300-liter long-range tanks beneath the wings and flame dampers increased drag and reduced the Bf 110's maximum speed to just 510 km/h at 5600 meters. The maximum speed of the Lancaster, the latest British heavy bomber, was 460 km/h. The speed differential between the Bf 110 and the newest British bombers was narrowing, making attacks difficult. As a result, night fighter victories dropped. Successes were often achieved at the cost of night fighter crews. The more powerful DB 605 engine was installed in the Bf 110 G, however the performance of the G-series did not live up to expectations. In spite of its more powerful engines, the Bf 110 G was slower than the single-engine Bf 109 E of 1940.

In spite of its shortcomings, the Bf 110 flew on. It formed the backbone of the German night fighter arm until the end of the war, mainly because no suitable replacement could be found. The Heinkel He 219, a promising night fighter, suffered mainly from a shortage of DB 603 engines. The German air command never viewed it as a true replacement for the Bf 110. The Heinkel type found itself in direct competition with the Messerschmitt Me 410 for the DB 603

Bf 110 F night fighters of III./NJG 5 in 1943. The aircraft belong to Lt. Fritz Carsten's 9. Staffel and were photographed in Königsberg during the unit's rest and refit. These were the first Bf 110s to be equipped with the FuG 202 radar. The Bf 110 formed the backbone of the German night fighter arm from 1940 until the end of the war.

engine. The allocation ratio was roughly eight to one in favor of the Me 410. The Me 410 was assigned a higher priority in every role. More Me 410 reconnaissance aircraft were built than He 219 night fighters. The German aviation industry failed to produce a really successful successor to the Bf 110 by the end of the war, and the gaps had to be filled by converted Ju 88 bombers.

Phoenix from the Ashes?

In the middle of 1942 there was an apparent comeback by the Fw 187. The RLM suddenly began showing interest in the aircraft again. Two years had been wasted. From 1940 to 1942 no development work on the type was permitted. Then, in May 1942, preliminary discussions were held on the potential use of the Fw 187 in a variety of roles. In June Professor Tank and his assistant Willi Kaether personally met with the responsible state secretary in the RLM. They showed him illustrations of the Fw 187 as a high-altitude fighter, heavy fighter and night fighter powered by DB 605 and DB 628 engines. To gain a first-hand impression of the aircraft, in late June *Major* Storp (RLM) went to Vaerløse with Tank and Kaether and flew the Fw 187. The first preliminary discussions in the *Technische Amt* took place on 1 July. In subsequent discussions the RLM showed interest in a heavy fighter version powered by Daimler Benz DB 605 engines. Soon afterwards the RLM contacted Kaether by telephone and instructed him to make the necessary modifications to an existing Fw 187. Focke Wulf proposed that two prototypes be built. The proposal was accepted. The airframes designated for conversion were the Fw 187 V5 (*Werknummer* 1976) and the Fw 187 B-0 (*Werknummer* 1977). As well, the two Fw 187 A-0s still in service in Vaerløse were to be ordered back for handling trials.

On 20 July 1942 Focke Wulf received the official development contract to redesign the Fw 187 as a so-called "*Kampf-Zerstörer*" to be powered by the new Daimler Benz DB 605 engine. Focke Wulf assumed from the development message sent on 7 August that the Fw 187 V5 would be converted and ready to fly by 31 October 1942 and the second aircraft, the Fw 187 V7 (B-0), by 30 November. Focke Wulf assigned this conversion plan Priority Level 2, behind the Fw 190 high-altitude fighter, which had top priority at that time. This relatively high priority level placed the Fw 187 conversions ahead of all other Fw 190 conversion plans, such as the photo reconnaissance version, and the Fw 191, which was then still in the test phase. Focke Wulf scheduled overtime and Sundays in order to have all the necessary drawings completed on time. The necessary component drawings had to be available to the assembly facility on time. The conversions were to take place in the prototype shop in Adelheide. The DB 605 engines for the two conversions were to be procured by 30 August and 30 September at the latest. Focke Wulf's schedule was a very tight one and planning was at an advanced stage.

Front view of the Fw 187.

The Daimler Benz DB 605 A engine was supposed to power the redesigned Fw 187. (DaimlerChrysler)

In mid-August 1942 Focke Wulf published an official specification for the redesigned Fw 187, the Fw 187 *Kampfzerstörer*. This resurgence of interest in the Fw 187 was a direct result of the massive problems being encountered with the Messerschmitt Me 210, which was supposed to replace the Bf 110. There was even talk of using Me 210 power plants for the Fw 187.

What had happened? The first Me 210, the V1, had first flown on 2 September 1939. Messerschmitt test pilot Hermann Wurster found that the aircraft suffered from serious directional and longitudinal instability. Messerschmitt's attempt to produce a capable multi-role aircraft seemed to have failed. Messerschmitt's original intention was to incorporate the lessons learned from the Bf 110 into the Me 210. It was to be more maneuverable and carry a heavier armament than its predecessor. The fuselage was short and the nose ended behind the propeller line. Unlike the Bf 110, the Me 210's forward-firing armament was housed in the forward fuselage instead of the fuselage nose. The aircraft was also designed to include an internal bomb bay covered by two doors. One extremely innovative feature was the aircraft's defensive armament. On each side of the fuselage just aft of the wing root there was an electrically-powered FDSLB-131/C remotely-controlled barbette mounting a 13-mm MG 131 machine-gun. The barbettes were controlled by joysticks operated by the observer and sighting was by means of a periscopic sight system.

In response to the poor handling of the Me 210 V1, the aircraft was fitted with a single fin and rudder in place of the original twin fins and rudders, but there was little improvement. The Me 210 V2 crashed on 5 September 1940. In spite of this bad omen, work on the project continued. The first Me 210 A-0 pre-production aircraft rolled from the production line in 1941, followed shortly by the Me 210 A-1. The aircraft were far from satisfactory, with poor handling characteristics the main problem. In spite of this the type was scheduled to enter mass production. Interestingly, Focke Wulf, which had earlier built the Bf 110, was scheduled to produce the Me 210

The Me 210 V1, D-AABF, still with its original twin fins and rudders. (EADS via Ebert)

under license using the Me 210 V5 as a prototype. As a result of production start-up of the new Fw 190 fighter, the contract for 140 Me 210 As was transferred to MIAG Brunswick.

What was the situation in 1942? In November 1938 the *Luftwaffe* General Staff had published a list of planned *Geschwader* numbers and the aircraft types which were to equip them. These plans called for eight *Geschwader* equipped with the heavy fighter version of the Me 210 and eight with the dive-bomber version. The reality in 1942 was quite different. After two and a half years of intensive development work the Me 210 still displayed directional and longitudinal instability as well as a fatal tendency to spin. These poor flight characteristics could not be rectified in spite of 16 prototypes, 8 pre-production aircraft and 13 A-1 production aircraft. Many Me 210s began to spin for no apparent reason. Even experi-

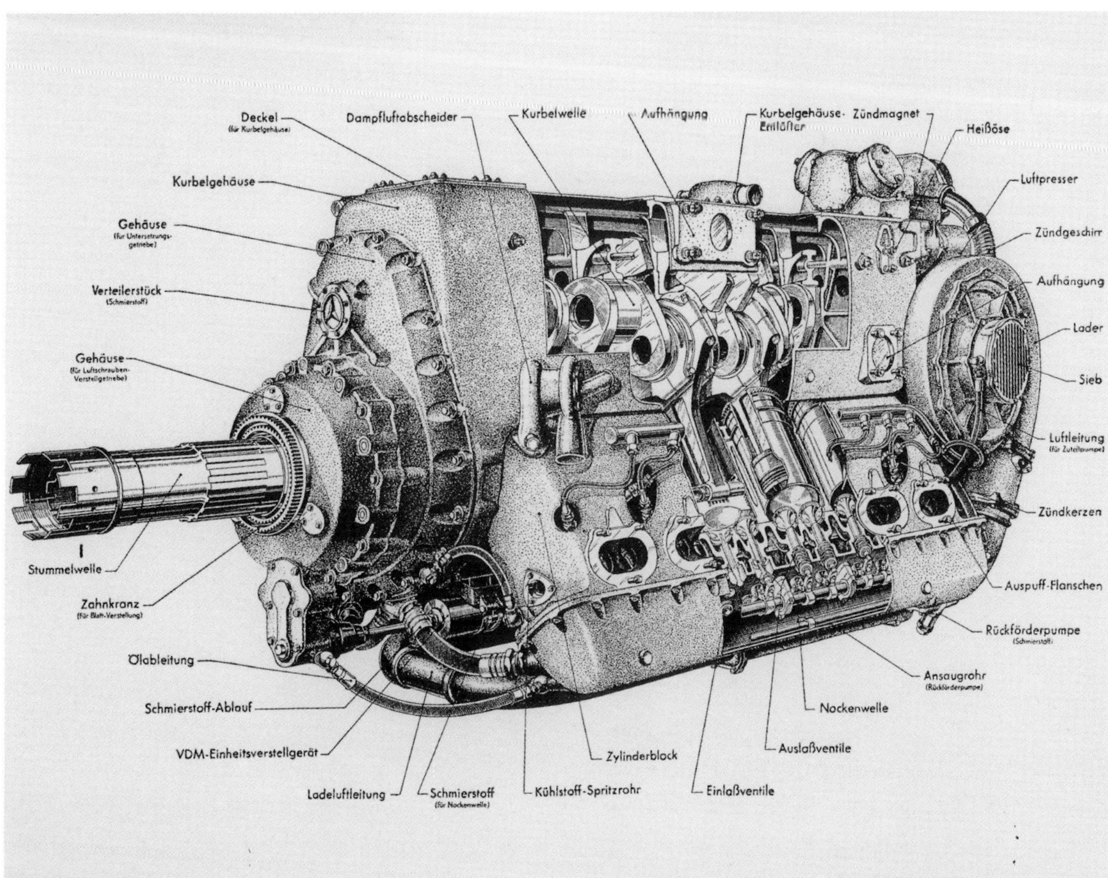

Drawing of the DB 605 A with component identification. (DaimlerChrysler Archive)

enced Messerschmitt test pilots lost their lives in Me 210 crashes. The well-known development engineer Ludwig Bölkow wrote that the Me 210 was a single summation of errors, even though another 58,500 hours of design work were expended by the autumn of 1940.

The Me 210 was supposed to have been available in large numbers for the Russian campaign in autumn 1941, however mass production had not yet begun. The misery reached the point that on 14 April 1942 *Reichsmarschall* Hermann Göring ordered a halt in production of the Me 210 and on 25 April ordered all work on the project to cease.

Messerschmitt was in crisis. One can imagine that all of the company's production resources had been readied for mass production and that the manufacture of components had begun. The *Luftwaffe* command's great trust in Messerschmitt's designs had been shaken for the first time. Prof. Messerschmitt was forced to step down as managing director of his company.

At that time, mid-1942, the failure of the Me 210 placed the *Luftwaffe*'s entire *Zerstörer* role in question. As well, the Me 210 had been designed as a multi-role aircraft capable of performing a variety of roles in addition to that of a *Zerstörer*. It was ultimately supposed to replace the Junkers Ju 87 dive-bomber, and its failure meant that the Ju 87 had to be kept in production. For the same reason the Bf 110, production of which was supposed to be phased out, had to be kept in production as a stop-gap measure. This would actually have been the hour of the Fw 187, which had none of the enormous technical problems of the Me 210.

In-flight photograph of Fw 187 "Yellow 7". Unlike the Me 210, the Fw 187 had no handling difficulties to overcome.

Although the Me 210 was a compact, streamlined design, its dangerous handling characteristics placed the lives of its pilots at risk.

Daimler-Benz	Leistungsblatt	DB 605 A-B B 4

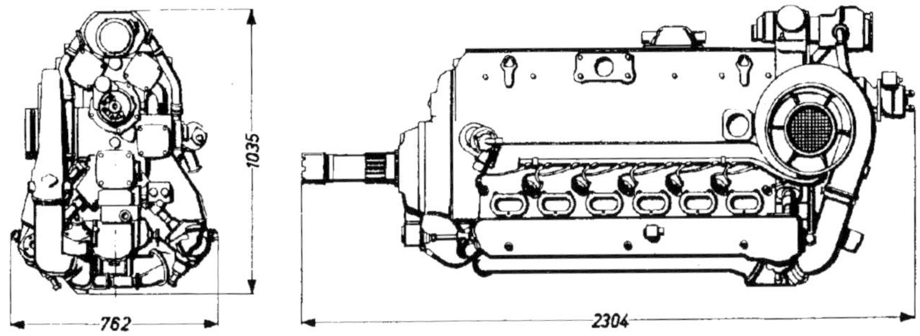

Höhe km	Leistungsstufe	PS	U/min	Ladedruck ata	Kraftstoffverbrauch g/PSh	l/h
0	Start-und Notleistung	1475	2800	1,42	235 + 10	480
0	Steig-und Kampfleistung	1310	2600	1,30	220 + 10	400
0	Höchstzul. Dauerleistung	1075	2300	1,15	215 + 10	320
5,7	Notleistung	1355	2800	1,42	235 + 10	450
5,8	Steig-und Kampfleistung	1250	2600	1,30	220 + 10	390
5,5	Höchstzul. Dauerleistung	1080	2300	1,15	215 + 10	320
5,7	Dauersparleistung	890	2100	1,05	205 + 10	250
10,0	Notleistung	790	2800	0,85	285 + 10	310

Untersetzung:		
	A	1:1,685 +)
	B	1:1,875 +)

Vergleichsgewicht: 720 kg + 3 %

Abzuführende Wärmemenge bei Steig-und Kampfleistung:

a. aus Schmierstoff max 65 000 kcal/h am Boden
" " " 43 000 " in Volldruckhöhe
b. " Kühlstoff " 340 000 " " "

Sonstige Vermerke:

Merkmale und Eignung:

Weiterentwicklung des DB 601 E mit nahezu gleichen Einbau- und Außenmaßen wie DB 601 E, jedoch mit größerem Hubvolumen, größerem Lader und höherer Drehzahl; dementsprechend größere Leistungen.

Druckkühlung.
Ölschleuder.
Gegenüber DB 601 E gekreuzte Kerzenlage, so daß sich günstiger Verbrauch, sowie größere Leistung ergibt.

Motor besonders geeignet für Weiterentwicklung des Jägers und Zerstörers, wenn vorher mit DB 601 E ausgerüstet.

+) konstruktiv ist auch 1:2,07 möglich, diese aus Beschaffungsgründen jedoch nicht freigegeben.

Unterschriften		Mappe Leistungsblätter Ausgabe: 601/LII 4.43
DAIMLER-BENZ A.G. Stgt.-Untertürkheim 60 AE	RLM GL/C-E3	9-605-6003

The DB 605 was derived from the DB 601 E and had almost identical dimensions. It was therefore ideally suited for developed versions of fighters and *Zerstörer* powered by the DB 601. (DaimlerChrysler Archive)

Performance Comparison Between the Redesigned Fw 187, the Me 210 C-1, and the Bf 110 G-3

As the following Specification shows, the Fw 187 was optimized for the new Daimler Benz DB 605 engine. Compared to the original Fw 187 of 1938, the fuselage was lengthened from 11.2 meters to 12.45 meters, while the wingspan was reduced from 15.48 to 15.30 meters. Gross weight increased from 5100 to 8200 kg. Armament kits (*Rüstsätze*) made it possible for the aircraft to be equipped with an additional armament of two MK 103 cannon, one 37-mm cannon or one 50-mm cannon beneath the fuselage. This made the aircraft suitable for the heavy fighter role. Focke Wulf made it clear that the Fw 187 could be used in a variety of other roles such as night fighter, bad-weather fighter and armed reconnaissance aircraft.

Designation Purpose	**Focke-Wulf Fw 187 (new)** Strategic Fighter	**Messerschmitt Me 210 C-1** Strategic Fighter	**Messerschmitt Bf 110 G-3** Heavy Fighter
Empty weight	5 660 kg	6 500 kg	5 850 kg
Gross weight	8 200 kg	9 600 kg	7 410 kg
Wingspan	15.30 m	16.34 m	16.25 m
Length	12.45 m	12.13 m	12.00 m
Height	3.35 m	4.28 m	4.13 m
Wing area	30.00 m^2	36.20 m^2	38.40 m^2
Wing loading	273.33 kg/m^2	265.19 kg/m^2	193 kg/m^2
Power Plants	2 x DB 605 A	2 x DB 605 B	2 x DB 605 B
Takeoff power	2 x 1475 PS	2 x 1475 PS	2 x 1475 PS
Fuel	B 4	B 4	B 4
Fuel capacity	1 250 l	2 400 l	1 270 l
with auxiliary tanks	2 150 l		3 070 l
Range	1 200 km	1 730 km	900 km
Range with auxiliary tanks	2 100 km		2 100 km
Takeoff distance	480 m	365 m	NA
Speed at ground level	547 km/h	478 km/h	500 km/h
Maximum speed	682 km/h	578 km/h	561 km/h
at maximum boost altitude	7.1 km	6.5 km	5.8 km
Rate of climb at ground level	13.0 m/s	8.7 m/s	11.0 m/s
Time to climb to 6000 m	5.7 min	–	7.1 min
Service ceiling	10.5 km	8.9 km	11.1 km
Fuselage armament	4 MG 151, 2 MG 131 1 MG 81	2 MG 151, 2 MG 131. 2 MG 17	2 MG 151, 4 MG 17 1 MG 81 Z
Bomb load	max. 2000 kg	max. 1800 kg	max. 2000 kg

The Me 210 V2 was fitted with a central fin instead of the previous twin fins and rudders. (EADS Unternehmensarchiv Ottobrunn via Ebert)

Also interesting is the performance of the Fw 187 without external stores but with outboard racks at a gross weight of 6620 kg. This was equivalent to the aircraft's weight with half its fuel used up. At ground level the Fw 187's estimated rate of climb was 18 m/s and at 2000 meters this increased to 19.2 m/s. Maximum speed at 7000 meters with emergency power was 694 km/h. These were extremely good figures for a twin-engined combat aircraft. With an externally-mounted 1000-kg bomb, maximum speed was 658 km/h at 7000 meters. This performance was achieved without MW 50 or GM1 boost. Neither the Bf 109 nor Fw 190 could equal the speed of the Fw 187.

The accompanying table compares various aspects of the Fw 187's performance with the Me 210 C-1 and the Bf 110 G-3. The Fw 187's better overall performance is clearly obvious. All three sub-types represented the latest developments in 1942 and all were powered by the DB 605 engine.

The Messerschmitt Me 210: the performance exhibited by the Me 210 was out of all proportion to the enormous amount of development work put into the project by Messerschmitt. Even though development of the Fw 187 was suspended for almost three full years, from 1939 to 1942, it proved relatively easy to adapt the aircraft to take more powerful engines in the form of the DB 605. The resulting machine was faster than the Me 210 with the same engines by almost 100 km/h at maximum boost altitude and 80 km/h at low altitude. The Fw 187 would have been faster than the Me 210 and at least equal, if not superior to, the de Havilland Mosquito, which was much feared at that time. Although the fuel capacity of the Fw 187 was half that of the Me 210, its maximum range was only 400 km less. This is an indication of just how advanced the design of the Fw 187 had been for the late 1930s. The Me 210 was never produced in large numbers, mainly because of its poor handling characteristics. When production ended in 1944, just 352 machines had been built.

From the 1944 the only remaining use for the Bf 110 was as a night fighter. This Bf 110 G-4 of III./NJG 6 landed in Dubendorf, Switzerland on 28 April 1944.

The Messerschmitt Bf 110 G-3: the failure of the Me 210 meant that the already obsolescent Bf 10 had to be kept in production in 1942. In an effort to improve the type's performance, more powerful DB 605 engines were installed. Armament consisted of four fixed MG 17 machine-guns and two MG 151 cannon in the fuselage nose and a flexibly-mounted MG 81 Z for the radio operator. This initial armament was inferior to that of the Fw 187. Later Bf 110s were fitted with a more powerful armament.

Compared to the Fw 187 with the same engines, the Bf 110 was approximately 130 km/h slower at the same altitude. It took the Bf 110 G-3 ten minutes to climb to 6000 m, almost twice as long as the Fw 187. It should be noted that the Bf 110 G-3's maximum speed of 565 km/h was inferior to that of British Hurricanes and Spitfires in service in 1939.

Specifications of the Fw 187 *Kampfzerstörer*

Until now the Specification of the reworked Fw 187 has never been published. It is presented here in its entirety for the first time. The performance of this aircraft, which Focke Wulf designated the Fw 187 New, will surprise many, for this redesigned version of the Fw 187 was capable of outstripping the latest versions of the Bf 109.

Description	
Type:	The Fw 187 is a twin-engined, cantilever low-wing monoplane. It is equipped with an hydraulically-retractable undercarriage and hydraulically-operated landing flaps.
Purpose:	*Kampfzerstörer*
Stress Group:	H5 without bombs; NA = 5 with 1000 kg external stores
Dimensions:	Wingspan = 15.3 m; Wing area = 30 m2
Crew:	Two
Power plants:	Two DB 605 (two BMW 801)
Normal gross weight:	8200 kg (with one 1000-kg bomb)
Estimated range:	1200 km without external tanks 2100 km with external tanks
Fuel system:	For range of 1200 km 1 protected tank in fuselage, contents 880 liters 2 protected tanks in wings, contents 210 liters each For range of 2100 km 2 jettisonable 900-liter tanks or 1 jettisonable tank
Armament:	4 x MG 151 fixed forward-firing, with 250 rounds per gun 2 x MG 131 fixed rearward-firing, with 450 rounds per gun 1 x MG 81 (rearward-firing) with 750 rounds
Aiming system:	Reflector sight for forward-firing weapons and bombing Rear-view periscope for fixed rearward-firing guns
External stores:	Maximum 2000 kg 1 x 1000 kg + 2 x 500 kg or 1 x 1000 kg + 4 x 250 kg or 10 x 50 kg or 10 x AB 23 or AB 24
Radio equipment:	FuG X P; Peil G VI Fu Bl 2 F Fu NG 101 FuG 25a
Armor:	16 kg armored windscreen 61 kg front-mounted 60 kg rear-mounted 30 kg radiator armor
Rüstsätze:	For carriage of 2 MK 103 cannon beneath fuselage
Remarks:	The aircraft can be equipped to serve as a night fighter, bad-weather fighter and armed reconnaissance aircraft.

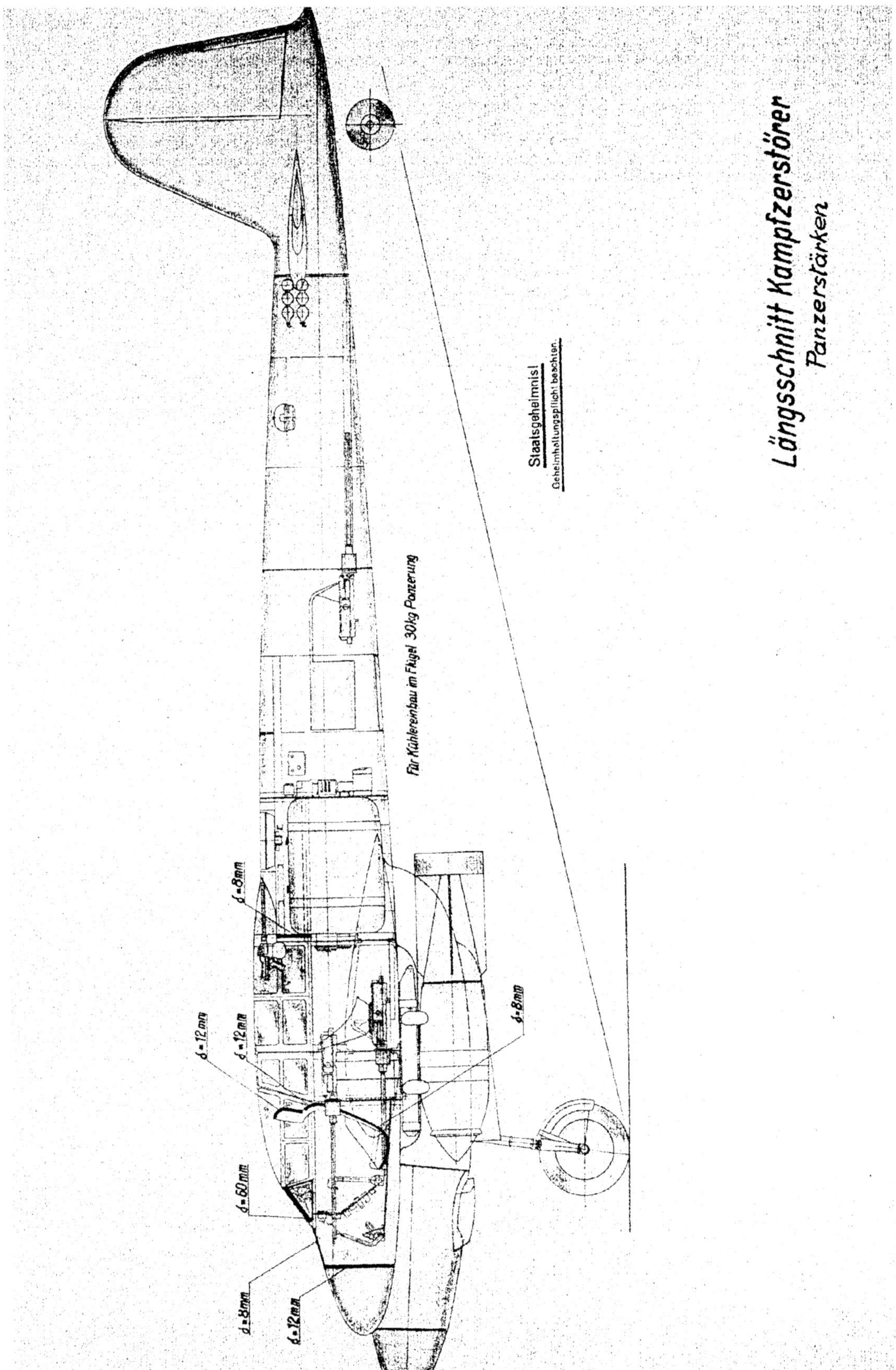
Längsschnitt Kampfzerstörer
Panzerstärken
Staatsgeheimnis!
Geheimhaltungspflicht beachten.
Für Kühlereinbau im Flügel 30kg Panzerung
d=8mm
d=12mm
d=12mm
d=8mm
d=60mm
d=8mm
d=12mm

Except for the new DB 605 engines, the redesigned Fw 187 would have looked almost identical to the Fw 187 A-0 from the front.

The Fw 187 also made an imposing impression from the rear. Note the aircraft's extremely slender fuselage.

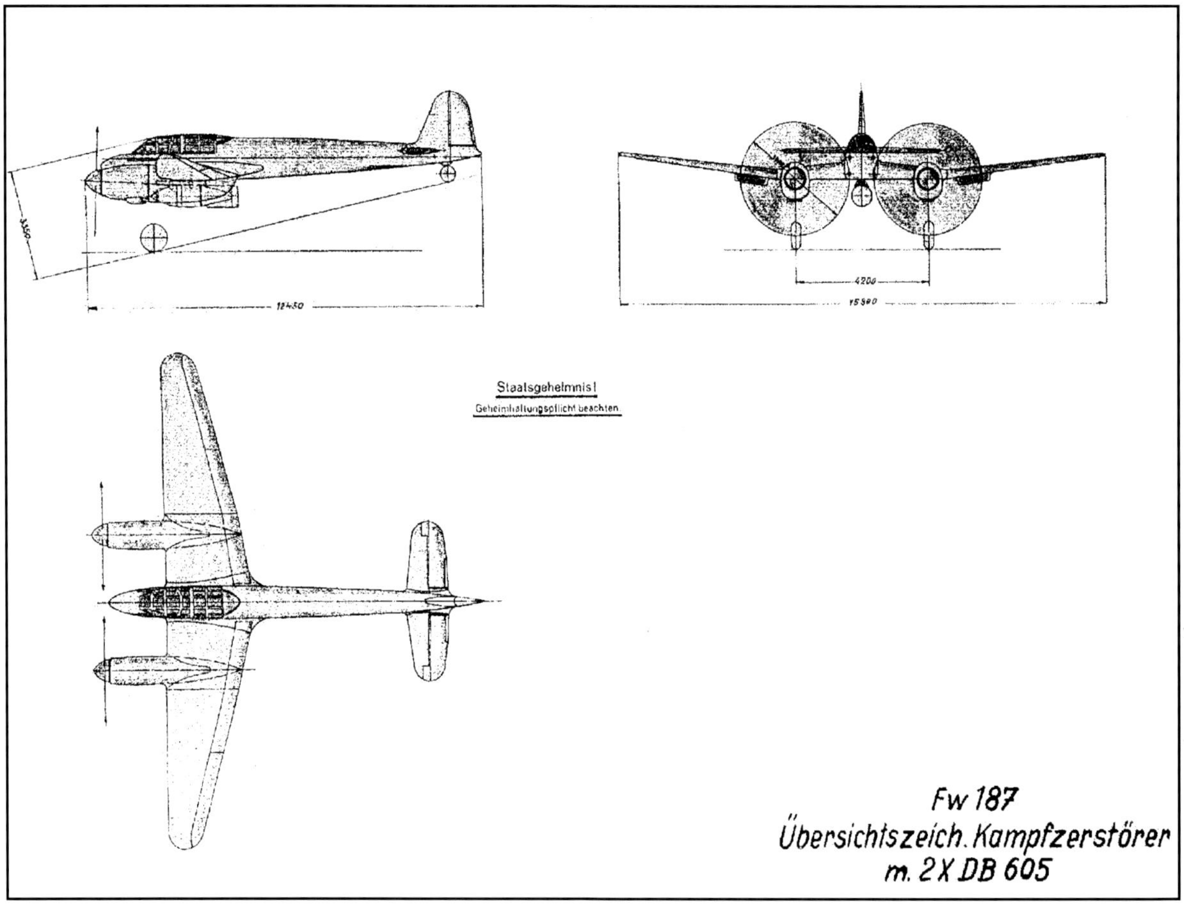

Three-view drawing of the Fw 187 high-speed *Kampfzerstörer* powered by two DB 605 engines. Although this new Fw 187 C version was developed four years after the A-series, differences are minor.

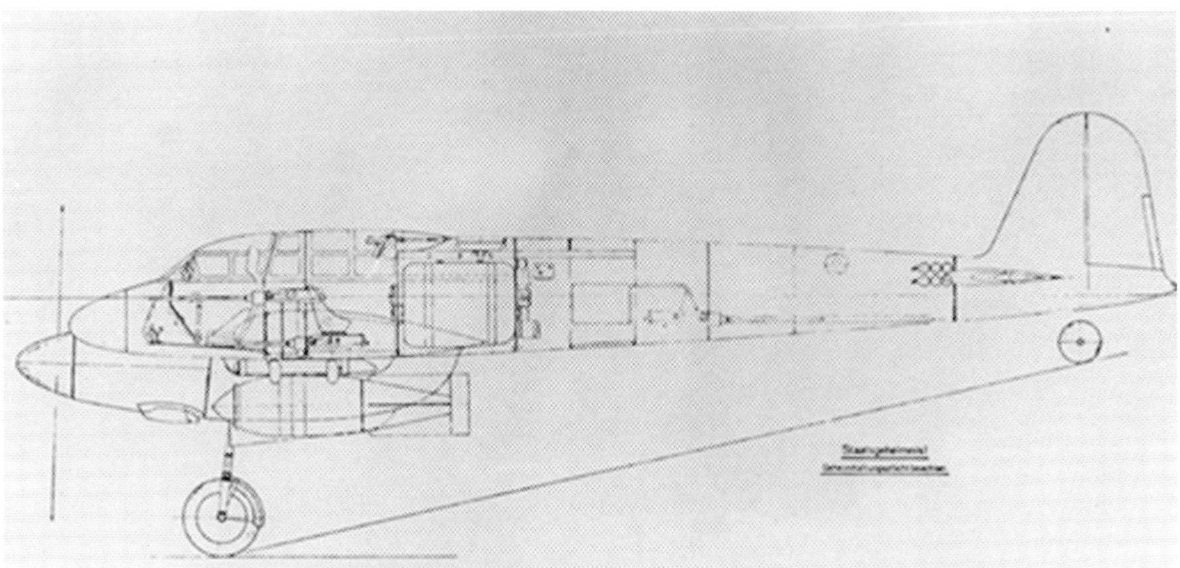

Side-view of the Fw 187 *Kampfzerstörer* with two Daimler Benz DB 605 engines and 1000-kg bomb load. Note the revised, bulged cockpit canopy of the C-version.

Table of Weights (all values in kg)

	Fw 187 with two DB 605		Fw 187 with two BMW 801	
Outer wing	354		354	
Inner wing	524		524	
Undercarriage gondolas	150		170	
Ailerons	28		35	
Landing flaps	29		37	
Wing	**1085**	**1085**	**1120**	**1120**
Forward fuselage	90		90	
Fuselage center-section	122		122	
Rear fuselage	111		111	
Fuselage fairing	5		5	
Fuselage fittings	36		36	
Armor	167		167	
Fuselage	**531**	**531**	**531**	**531**
Horizontal stabilizer	77		95	
Vertical stabilizer	46		53	
Tail Surfaces	123	123	151	151
Controls in cockpit	14		14	
Controls in fuselage	18		18	
Controls in tail surfaces	18		18	
Controls wing	19		19	
Controls	69	69	69	69
Wheels 840x300	92		92	
Shock struts with fairings	199		210	
Hydraulics	53		53	
Tailwheel	34		36	
Undercarriage	**378**	**378**	**391**	**391**
Airframe		**2186**		**2244**
Engine and accessories	1559		2108	
Coolant and oil in engines	62		70	
Motor mounts	68		86	
Engine nacelles	12		12	
Engine control rods	82		90	
Oil cooler and contents	126		-	
Radiator and contents	32		-	
Engine piping	67		50	
Exhaust system	20		53	
Propellers and spinners	344		352	
Fuselage fuel tank	77		77	
Wing fuel tanks	74		74	
Oil tank	35		35	
Coolant tank	32		35	
Fuel and oil system	40		-	
Armor	-		39	
Power plants	**2630**	**2630**	**3086**	**3086**

Table of Weights (continued)

	Fw 187 with two DB 605		Fw 187 with two BMW 801	
Power plants	**2630**	**2630**	**3086**	**3086**
Ignition system	39		39	
Engine instruments	10		10	
Propeller pitch control mechanism	10		10	
Flight instruments	66		6	
Navigation equipment	25		25	
Intercom	1		1	
Power Supply	55		55	
Electric lighting	2		2	
Lines and housings	75		75	
Permanent equipment	223	223	223	223
Empty Weight		**5039**		**5553**
Autopilot	20		20	
Safety and rescue equipment	20		20	
Radio equipment	141		141	
Weapons installation:	392		392	
4 MG 151 (fixed forward-firing)				
2 MG 131 (fixed rearward-firing)				
1 MG 81 (flexibly-mounted, rearward-firing)				
External stores:				
Accessories	24		24	
Bomb racks	40		40	
Additional equipment	637	637	637	637
Equipped weight		5658		6190
1 pilot	100		100	
1 crewman	100		100	
Fuel	960		960	
Oil	70		70	
Ammunition	306		306	
Bombs	1000		1000	
Additional Load	**2536**	**2536**	**2536**	**2536**
Normal Gross Weight		**8194**		**8726**
		ca. **8200**		ca. **8730**

Photograph of an Fw 187 A-0 in service with a Focke-Wulf industry defense flight.

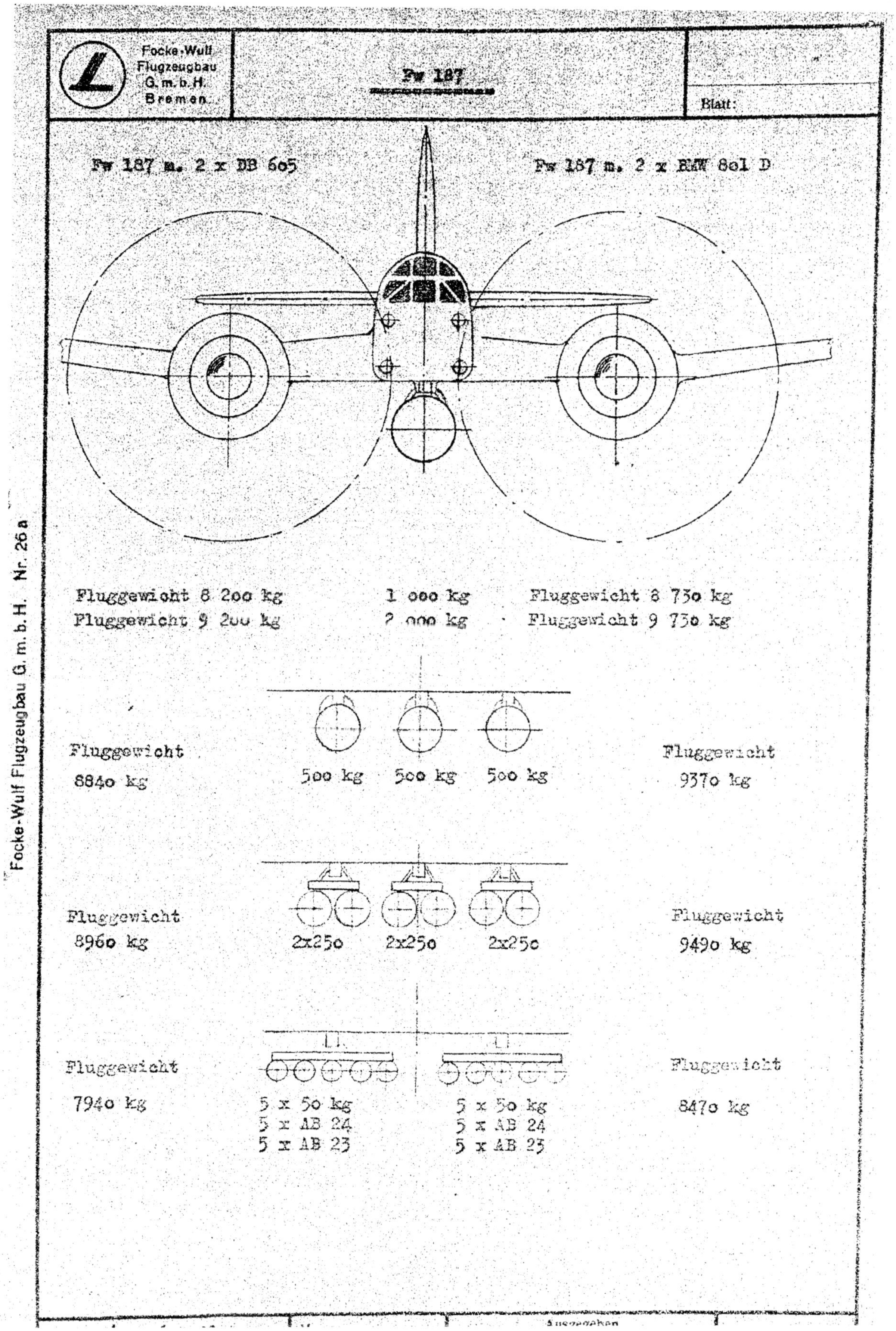
Focke-Wulf Flugzeugbau G.m.b.H. Bremen
Fw 187
Blatt:
Fw 187 m. 2 x DB 605
Fw 187 m. 2 x BMW 801 D
Fluggewicht 8 200 kg
Fluggewicht 9 200 kg
1 000 kg
2 000 kg
Fluggewicht 8 730 kg
Fluggewicht 9 730 kg
Fluggewicht
8840 kg
500 kg
500 kg
500 kg
Fluggewicht
9370 kg
Fluggewicht
8960 kg
2x250
2x250
2x250
Fluggewicht
9490 kg
Fluggewicht
7940 kg
5 x 50 kg
5 x AB 24
5 x AB 23
5 x 50 kg
5 x AB 24
5 x AB 23
Fluggewicht
8470 kg
Focke-Wulf Flugzeugbau G.m.b.H. Nr. 26 a

Type Sheet

Fw 187 *Kampfzerstörer* with two DB 605 A-C

Power plants	2 x DB 605 A-C (B4 fuel) reduction ratio 1 : 1.875
Takeoff power	2 x 1,475 h.p. at 2,800 rpm
Climb and combat power (low level)	2 x 1,310 h.p. at 2,600 rpm
Climb and combat power (high altitude)	2 x 1,350 h.p. at 2,600 rpm at 7000 m

Propellers	3.40 meters diameter, three blade
Wingspan	15.3 meters
Length	12.45 meters
Height	3.35 meters
Wing area	30 m^2

Armament A,B,C,D (see Specification)

Equipped weight	5660 kg
Crew (2)	200 kg
Ammunition	306 kg
Fuel (9.74 kg/l)	960 kg
Oil (9.93 kg/l)	70 kg
Bombs	1000 kg
Gross weight	8200 kg

Maximum speed	N (h.p.)	A (m)	
	2 x 1,310	0	547 km/h
	2 x 1,450	3300	632 km/h
	2 x 1,290	7100	682 km/h
	2 x 980	9000	658 km/h

Cruising speed and	N (h.p.)	b (kg/h.p.)	H (m)	Cruise	Range
Range (estimated)	2 x 600	.210	0	397 km/h	1330 km
	2 x 720	.210	1000	440 km/h	1210 km
	2 x 855	.210	4000	520 km/h	1200 km
	2 x 810	.210	6000	539 km/h	1250 km

Service ceiling G_A	10500 m
Service ceiling G_M	12000 m

Time to climb	A = 1000 m	0.9 min.
	A = 2000 m	1.7 min.
	A = 4000 m	3.6 min.
	A = 6000 m	5.7 min.

Takeoff Distance /Paved 480 m / 700 m

Landing speed at 6500 kg (without bombs)	143 km/h
Wing loading	217 kg/m^2
Initial rate of climb (aircraft in takeoff configuration)	7.7 m/s
Climbing speed	185 km/h

Rate of climb with undercarriage retracted, landing flaps in climb position (at low level)	13 m/s
Climbing speed	285 km/h

Two mechanics feed belts of ammunition into the fuselage machine-guns of the Fw 187. The new Fw 187 C would have carried a much heavier armament (Petrick)

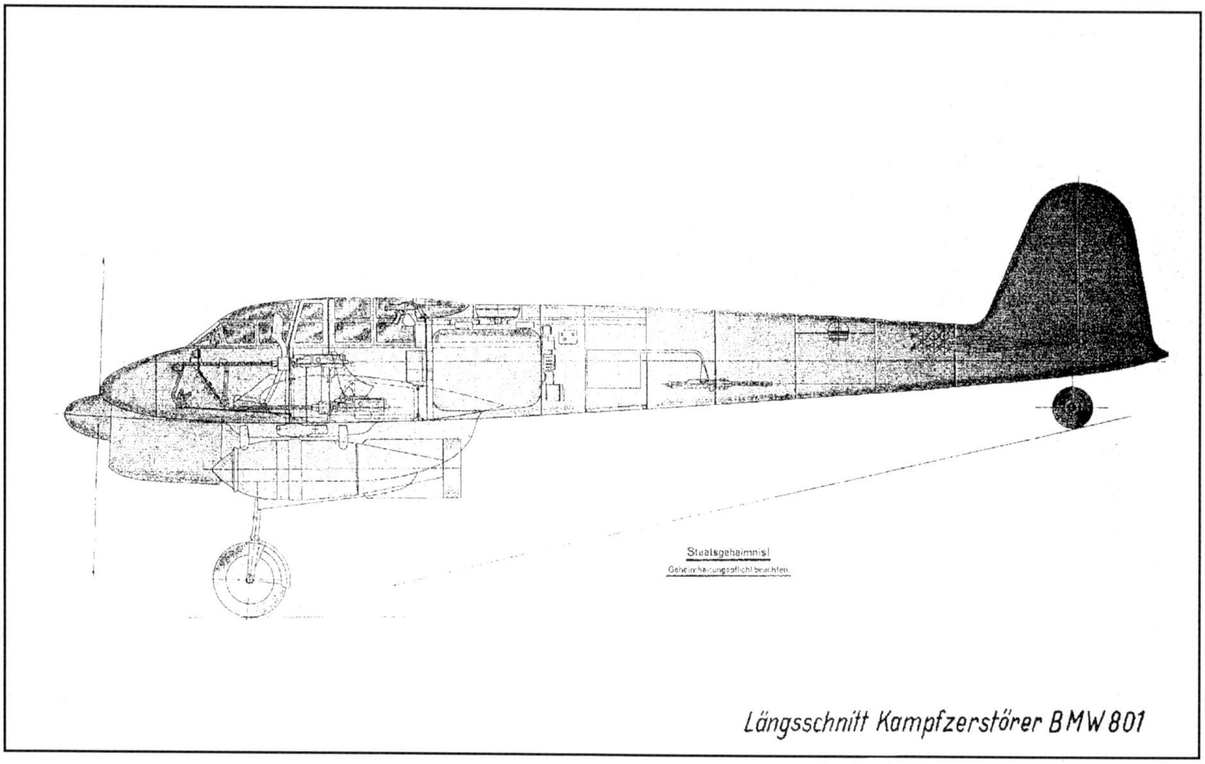

An alternative version of the Fw 187 was proposed with BMW 801 engines. The increased weight of the engines would have been offset by their greater horsepower. No RLM contract was forthcoming for this promising version.

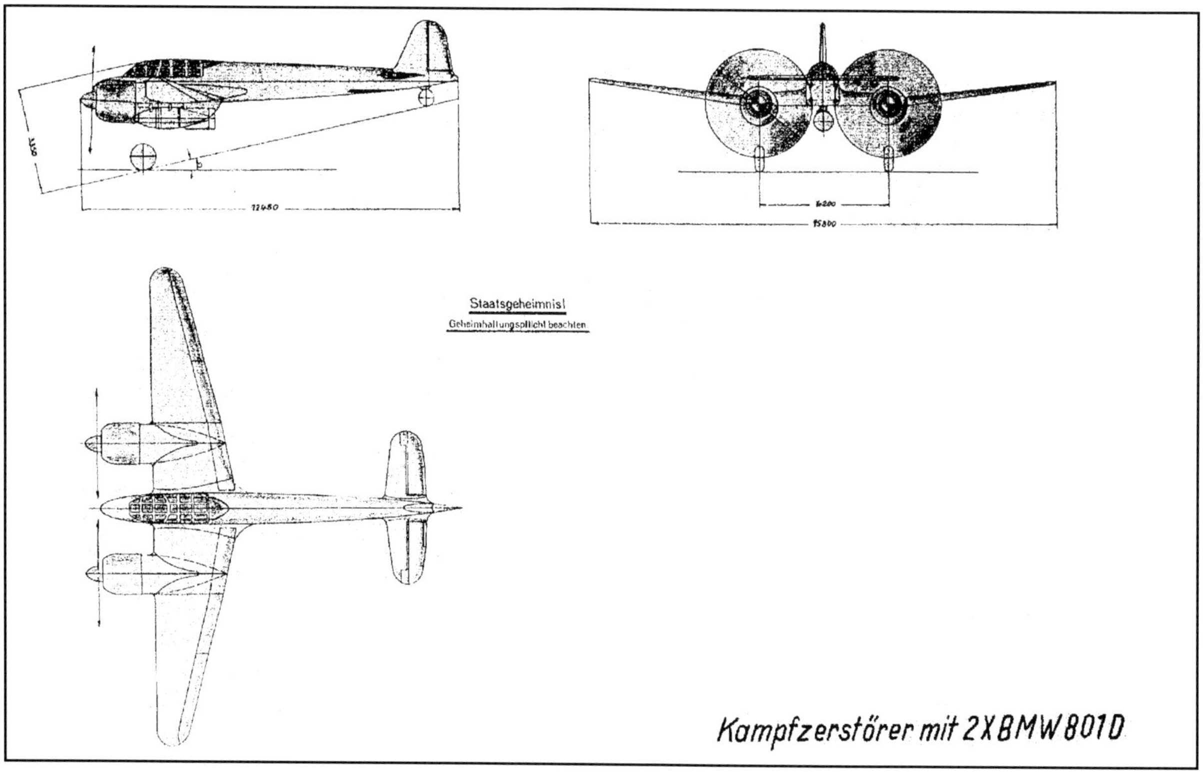

The redesigned Fw 187 *Kampfzerstörer* with two BMW 801 engines and a 1000-kg bomb load. The bulkier radial engines changed the slender appearance of the aircraft, however performance would have been similar to that of the DB 605-powered version.

Three photographs of Fw 187 A-0s in service with the industry defense unit.

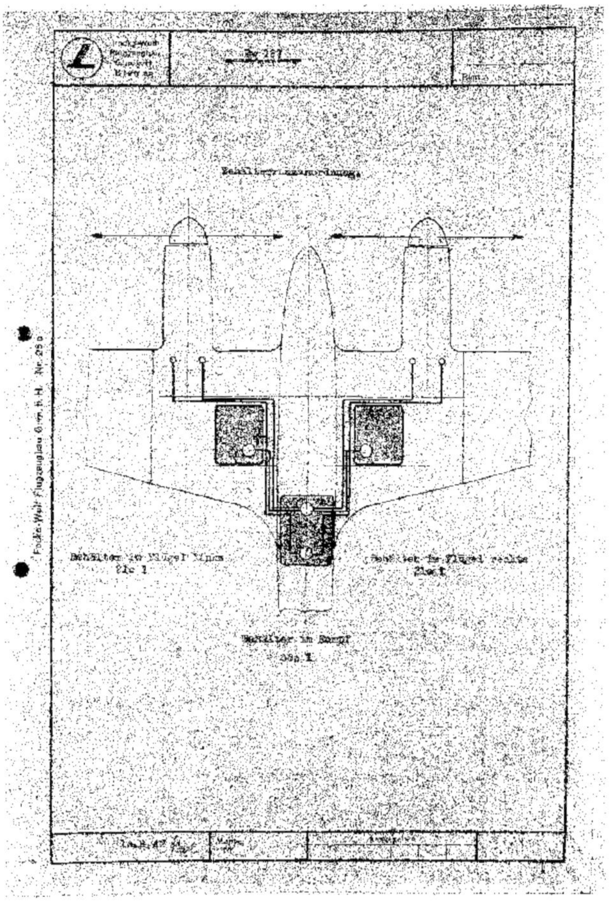

This 1300-liter fuel tank would have increased the range of the Fw 187 to a maximum of 1330 km. The fuel system would not have differed significantly from that of the A and B series.

The filler cap for the Fw 187's fuselage tank was covered by two access flaps. (EADS Unternehmensarchiv Bremen)

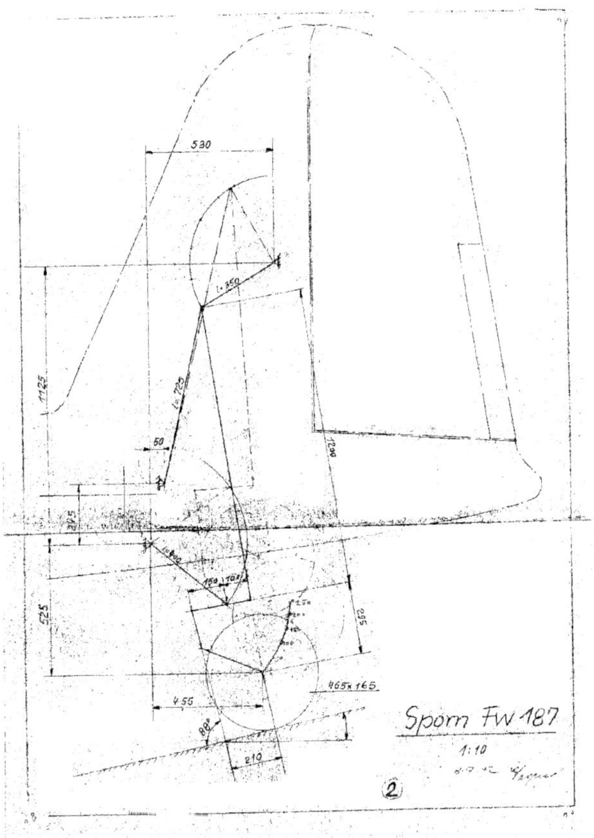

The tailwheel was revised twice during the Fw 187 C's brief design phase. The tail surfaces of the Fw 187 C were largely unchanged. The ultimate configuration date was 11/8/42.

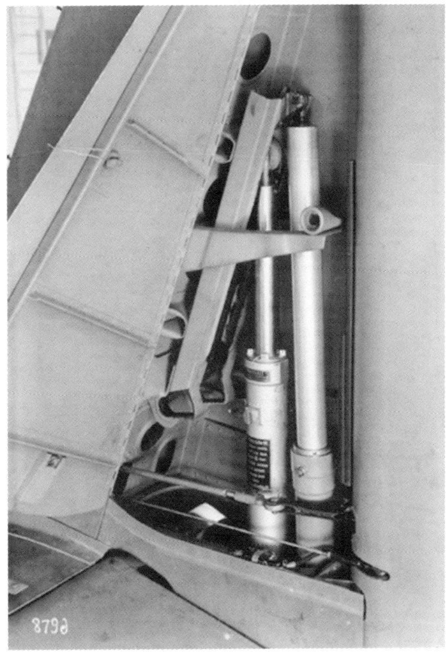

Above: Original tailwheel mechanism of the Fw 187 A.

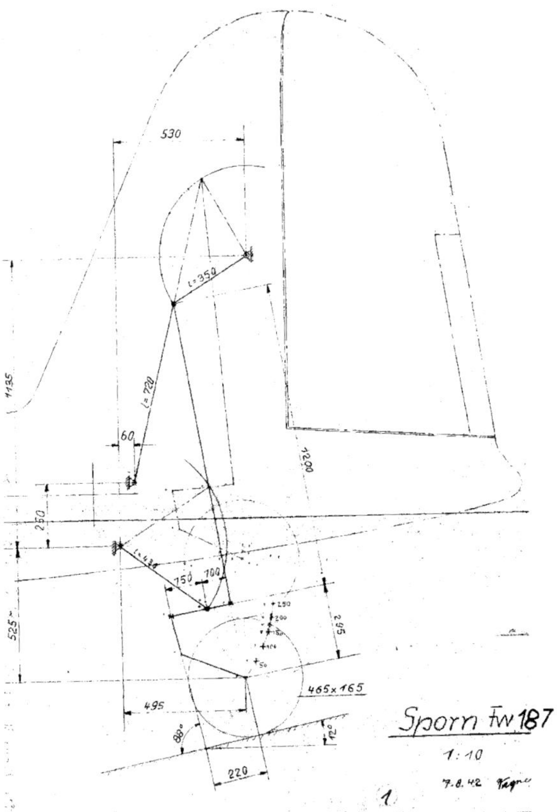

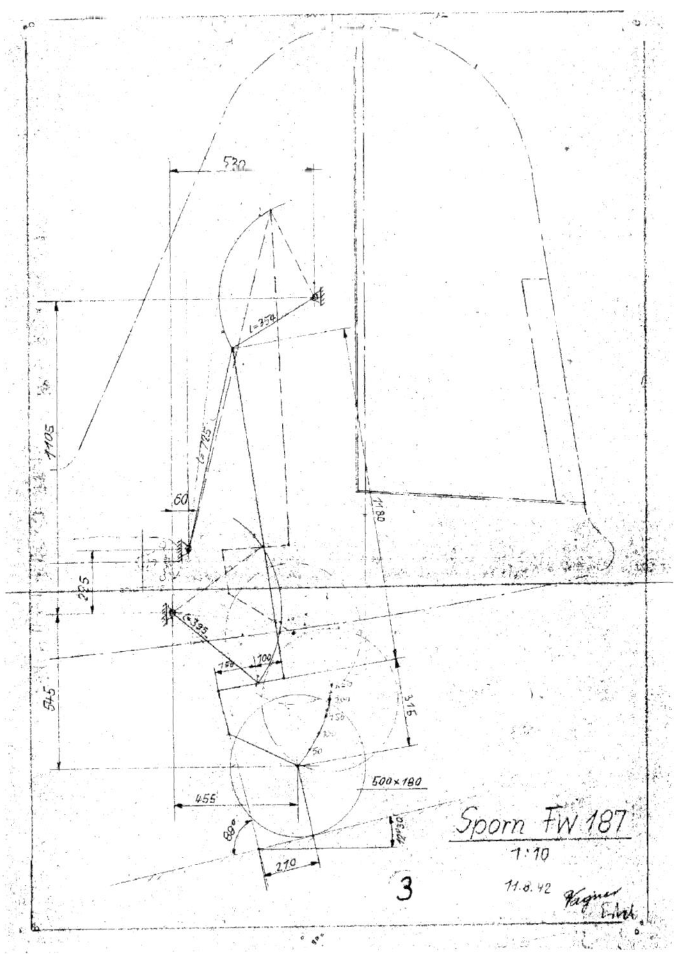

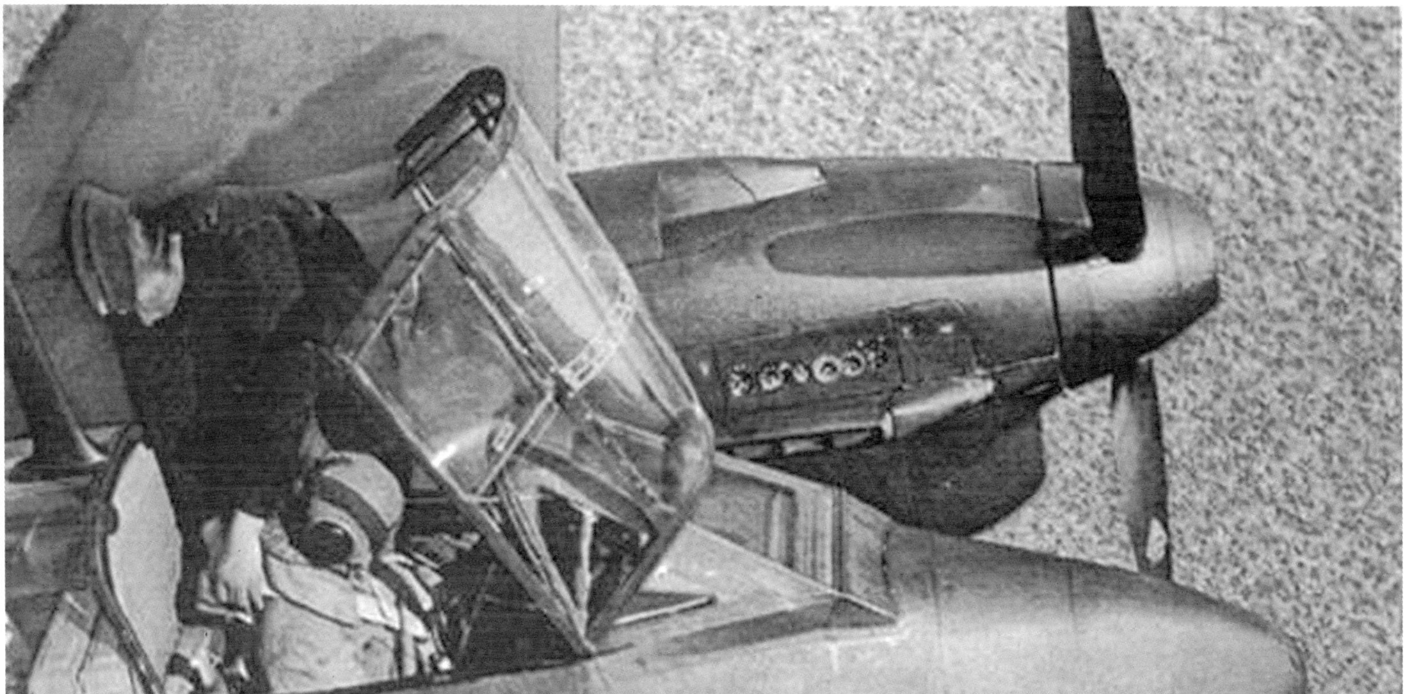

Above: This photograph provides an excellent view of the engine instruments installed in the inner nacelles of the Fw 187. (Focke Wulf)

The He 100 and Fw 187 shared a number of characteristics. Both were very near to the hearts of their designers. Both were equipped with evaporation cooling systems in an attempt to increase speed. Both types failed to enter large-scale production. The few pre-production examples of both types were used in industry defense units and were exploited for propaganda purposes, as seen here.

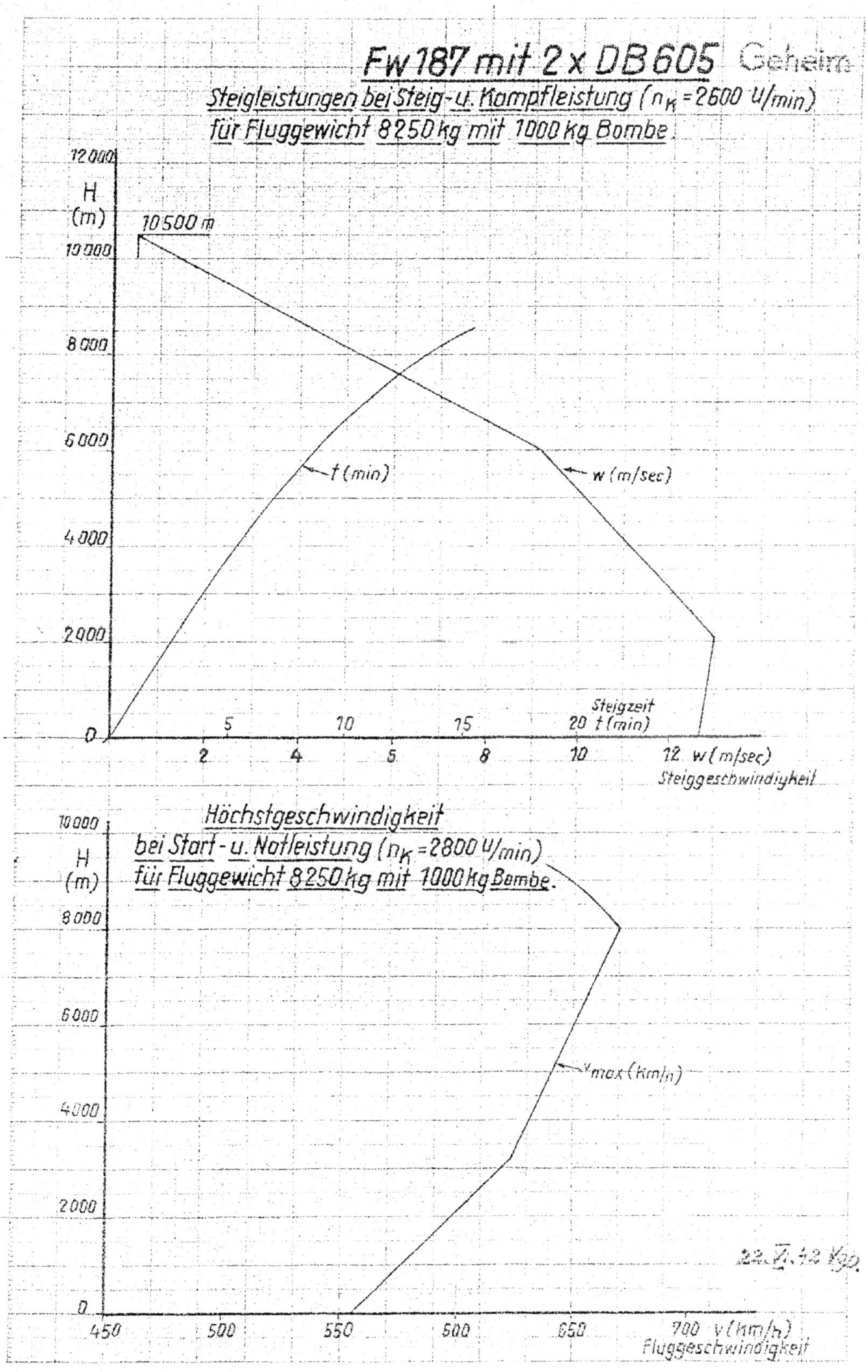

With a 1000-kg bomb load, the maximum speed of the Fw 187 C was 670 km/h at an altitude of 8000 meters.

Preparing for Production

On 20 July 1942 Focke Wulf received the development contract to prepare the Fw 187 for production and the entire organization was immediately set in motion. Focke Wulf estimated that 373,700 engineer hours and 223,500 man hours would be required to design the Fw 187 C-0 and ready it for production. Focke Wulf's proposal to the RLM in 1940 included total costs of 3,362,000 Reichsmark. At that time the Fw 187 was a pure light-metal aircraft. When the project was restarted, Focke Wulf was instructed to investigate the possible use of materials other than light metals. The cost of these investigations was included in Focke Wulf's proposal. The RLM was promised that all design work would be completed by early 1943. Acceptance checks on the first aircraft to be converted, the Fw 187 V5, were carried out on 12 August 1942. The aircraft was found to be acceptable for the most part. Some pieces were missing, as they had been sent to Vaerløse as replacement parts (landing flaps, for example). The V7, which had never flown, was in poor condition. It was only 80% complete and was badly rusted, as the aircraft had been left outside for a long period as part of evaporation tests. Some components of this machine had also been removed for the two Fw 187 A-0s in Vaerløse. In fact, *Werknummer* 1977 was in such poor condition that a proposal was made to convert one of the A-0 aircraft in Vaerløse instead. This proposal was rejected, because conversion costs would have been greater and because there were differences in wing leading edge sweep between the A-0 and the V7, which would have required new calculations. As the outer wings for *Werknummer* 1977 could not be found, a decision was made to use the wings from *Werknummer* 1979. For testing, the following designations were selected: *Werknummer* 1976 would be the Fw 187 V5/U1, *Werknummer* 1977 would be the Fw 187 V7/U1 and the first prototype would be the Fw 187 V8. The pre-production aircraft would be designated Fw 187 C-0. The designation Fw 187_{Br} was assigned to the static test airframe. It was also decided that construction of the initial production series would proceed in parallel with the pre-production series. This reflected the enormous pressure being applied by the RLM. The following contracts were issued for the Fw 187:

1. Modification and production readiness for the Fw 187 C-0 production drawings. (10 07 080).
2. Handling trials with both Fw 187 aircraft returned from Denmark. (10 07 081)
3. Construction of a Fw 187_{Br} static test airframe (for DB 605). (10 07 082)
4. Redesign and conversion, plus construction, of additional jigs for conversion to the DB 605-powered Fw 187. (10 07 083)
5. Design and construction of a fuselage mock-up of the DB 605-powered Fw 187. (10 07 084)
6. Conversion to materials other than light metals and associated experiments for the DB 605-powered Fw 187. (10 07 085)
7. Conversion of Fw 187 aircraft Werk-Nr. 1976 with DB 605 power plants. (50 07 012)
8. Conversion of Fw 187 Werk-Nr. 1977 (second conversion aircraft) to the DB 605.

It was initially planned to use the Daimler Benz DB 605 power plants of the Me 210 to power the Fw 187 production series. Various officials in the *Technische Amt* complained, however, and a decision was made to use the Bf 109 G power plant, also a DB 605. This meant that Focke Wulf would have to modify or redesign much of the engine cowling. Other significant modifications which had to be made to bring the V5/U1 and V7/U1 prototypes up to C-0 standards were: lengthening of the fuselage by one meter, reinforcement of the fuselage, installation of trim weights, conversion of the inner ailerons to landing flaps because of the underwing radiator installation, and strengthening of the outer wings as a result of the underwing radiator installation. Radio equipment for the *Kampfzerstörer* version would included the FuG 10P, FuG 16, FuG

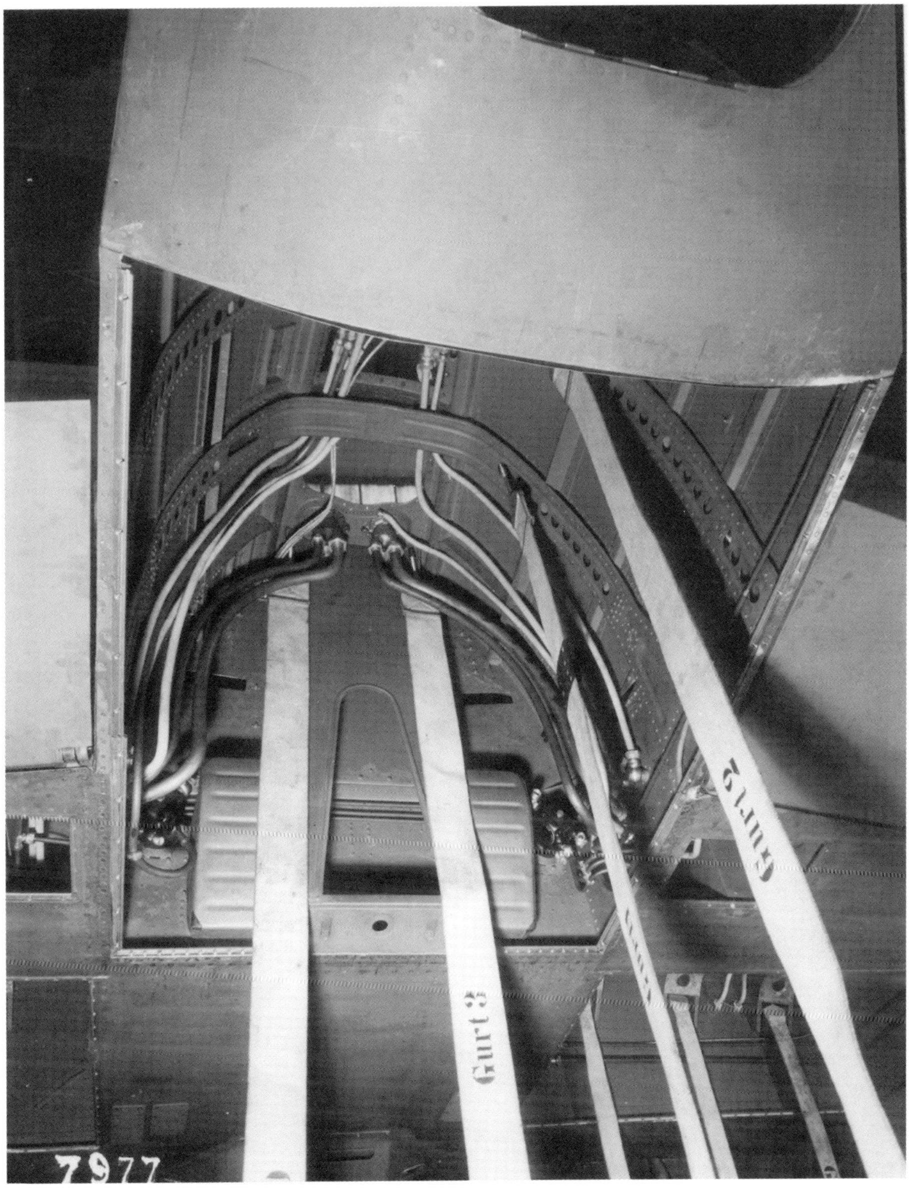

Fuselage structure of the Fw 187.

25a, Peil G6, FuBl 2f, and FuG 101 for voice communications. Additional equipment for the night fighter role consisted of the FuG 15 and FuG 202 (Lichtenstein C-1). The V5/U1 and V7/U1 would be equipped with the FuG 17, as the FuG 15 was not yet available. It was also planned to install the FuG 101 in the V7/U1 for operating trials. No armament was planned for either prototype. The first flight of the V5/U1 was scheduled for the end of October 1942, a date which had to be met, while the V7/U1's first flight was set for the end of November 1942. The first flight of the Fw 187 V8 preproduction aircraft was scheduled for early 1943.

Construction of the fuselage mock-up began in the mock-up shop in Bad Eilsen on 4 August 1942. The mock-up in fact consisted of three mock-ups, namely a cockpit mock-up, an inner wing mock-up for cooling system installation experiments, and a mock-up of the rear fuselage to show the fuselage extension. The fuselage mock-up was to be equipped with all the planned technical installations and equipment. The FuG 202 air intercept radar was also installed. A mock-up of the FuG 212 installation was also requested for a possible installation of that equipment. The framework was completed on 22 August and the deadline for official inspection was early September.

Investigations into Possible Conversion of the Fw 187 for the High-Altitude Fighter Role

With work to prepare the Focke Wulf Fw 187 *Kampfzerstörer* for production in full swing, the RLM requested that the company also give serious consideration to high-altitude and night fighter versions of the aircraft. The results of these investigations are reproduced below:

"Investigations into fighter aircraft have revealed that significant improvements in rate of climb and service ceiling with adequate armament cannot be achieved by a single-engine aircraft using available engines.

Considerations lead to a twin-engined aircraft, as such have significantly lower power loadings. For this reason, the Fw 187 was examined for suitability for conversion into a (a) high-altitude fighter and (b) a night fighter.

It was found that the few available examples of the Fw 187, which was designed as a *Zerstörer*, are capable of meeting all the requirements of a high-altitude and night fighter. The existing wing loading and aspect ratio are completely acceptable for the new role, consequently no fundamental design changes are required.

Two DB 605 engines were selected as power plants because of their performance characteristics. The engine system of the DB 605-powered Bf 109 G will be used. The necessary modifications in the are of the wing are minor, because the airframe attachment points have been designed for the DB 601.

In contrast to the Fw 187 V1 to V5, ducted radiators can be installed between the fuselage and engine nacelles instead of ventral or longitudinal radiators. The resulting modifications to the wing are also minor as there are already suitable cutouts in the wings.

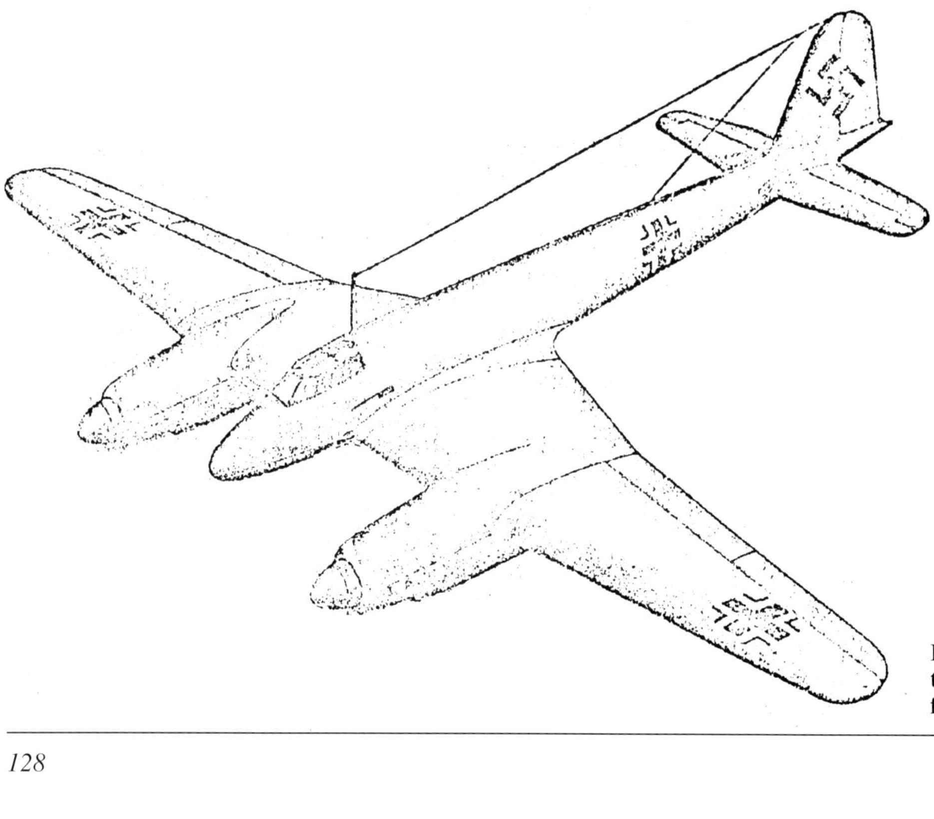

In spite of its poor quality, this drawing reveals the elegant shape of the proposed high-altitude fighter version of the Fw 187.

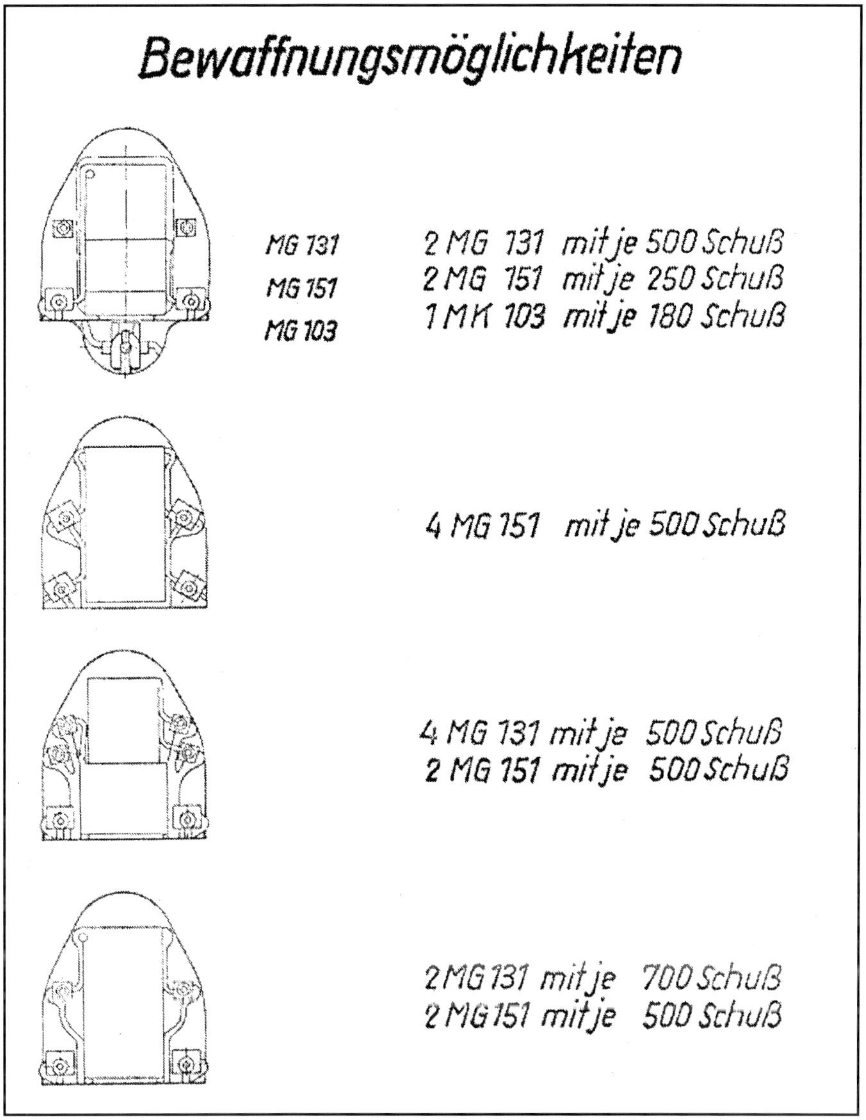

Armament combinations.

The fuel tanks previously installed in the inner wings will have to be removed. As the aircraft is to be produced as a single-seater, removal of the observer's position will result in space for an additional fuselage tank with a capacity of approximately 250 liters. Design drawings for this are already available.

For handling reasons the fuselage will have to be extended by approximately one meter. This extension affects only the simple end piece between Frames 15 and 27, which houses little equipment. The resulting gross weigh is 6050 kg.

The 815x290 wheels of the Fw 187 will no longer suffice, given the increased weight, and an 840x290 wide-rim wheel is proposed. The slightly increased dimensions of the new wheels will require some modification of the existing undercarriage.

Planned armament consists of:

(a) High-Altitude Fighter
2 x MG 131 with 700 rounds per gun
2 x MG 151 with 500 rounds per gun

(b) Night Fighter
4 x MG 151 with 500 rounds per gun

The existing arrangement of weapons will be retained. Since, apart from the fuselage extension, the aerodynamically-effective components will be retained, it can be expected that the developed aircraft will retain the proven good handling characteristics of the Fw 187.

Investigations have also revealed that conversion of the Fw 187 can be undertaken in a short time with little design work required.

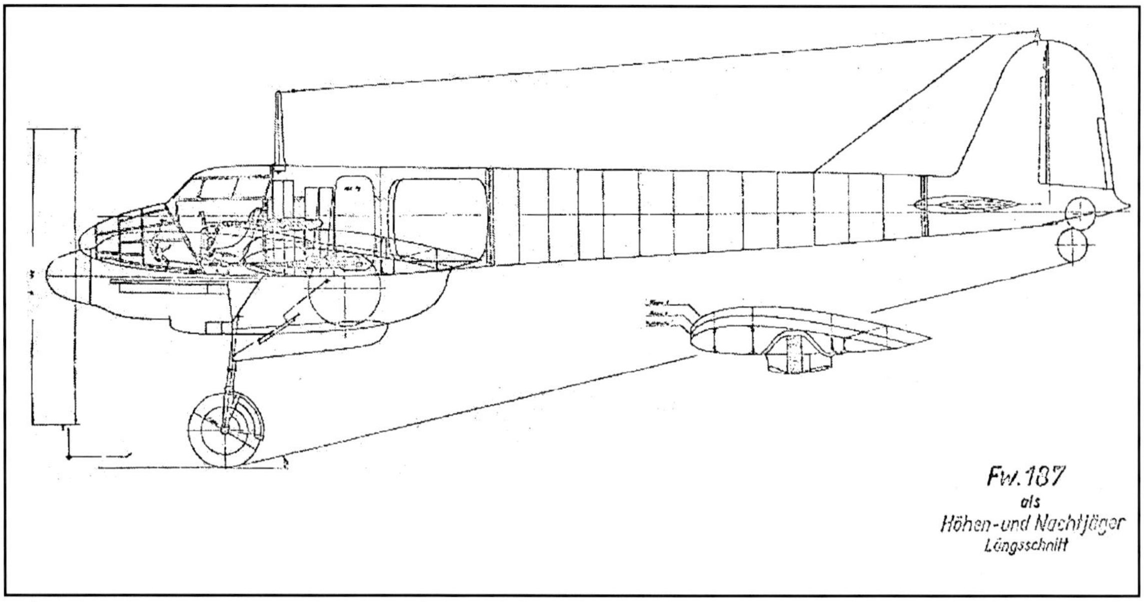

Side-view of the Fw 187 high-altitude and night fighter.

Delivery Possibilities

Completion of the reworked construction drawings by November 1942, provided that all designers and other personnel loaned to other companies are returned.

Construction of four prototypes for the purpose of eliminating drawing errors from the construction drawings and for new tests of the airframe and power plants (Bf 109 engine, airframe already tested) by mid-1943.

Delivery of first production aircraft in early 1944.

Summary:

It has been determined that the few operational examples of the Fw 187, which was originally developed as a *Zerstörer*, are capable of meeting all the requirements of a high-altitude and night fighter following the installation of more powerful engines with very minor modifications. The handling characteristics, wing loading and general layout of the Fw 187 are completely adequate for these new roles. Use of the DB 605 power plant from the Bf 109 is given."

At the time of the Fw 187 high-altitude fighter projections in mid-1942, Focke Wulf already had some experience in the development of high-altitude fighters. For two years Focke Wulf had been attempting to develop a high-altitude version of the Fw 190 fighter, but with little success. It was not for nothing that Focke Wulf wrote of the better suitability of a twin-engined aircraft for the high-altitude role at the beginning of this description.

In Focke Wulf's estimation the risks associated with developing the Fw 187 as a high-altitude fighter were low. As mentioned in the original text, there were still several Fw 187s flying, for example in the Vaerløse Aerial Gunnery School, which could be seen as proof of the quality of the original design.

Weight Table

Fuselage	300 kg
Undercarriage	450 kg
Tail section	170 kg
Control surfaces	45 kg
Wing	715 kg
Power plants	2700 kg
Permanent equipment	115 kg
Other equipment	170 kg
SO equipment	240 kg
Equipped weight	**4905 kg**
Crew (one)	100 kg
Fuel tank I	460 kg
Fuel tank II	180 kg
Oil	70 kg
2 x 700 rounds MG 131	140 kg
2 x 500 rounds MG 151	195 kg
Loading	1145 kg
Gross weight	**6050 kg**

Focke Wulf began high-altitude fighter development with the Fw 190. Seen here is the first Fw 190 A-3/U7 high-altitude fighter.

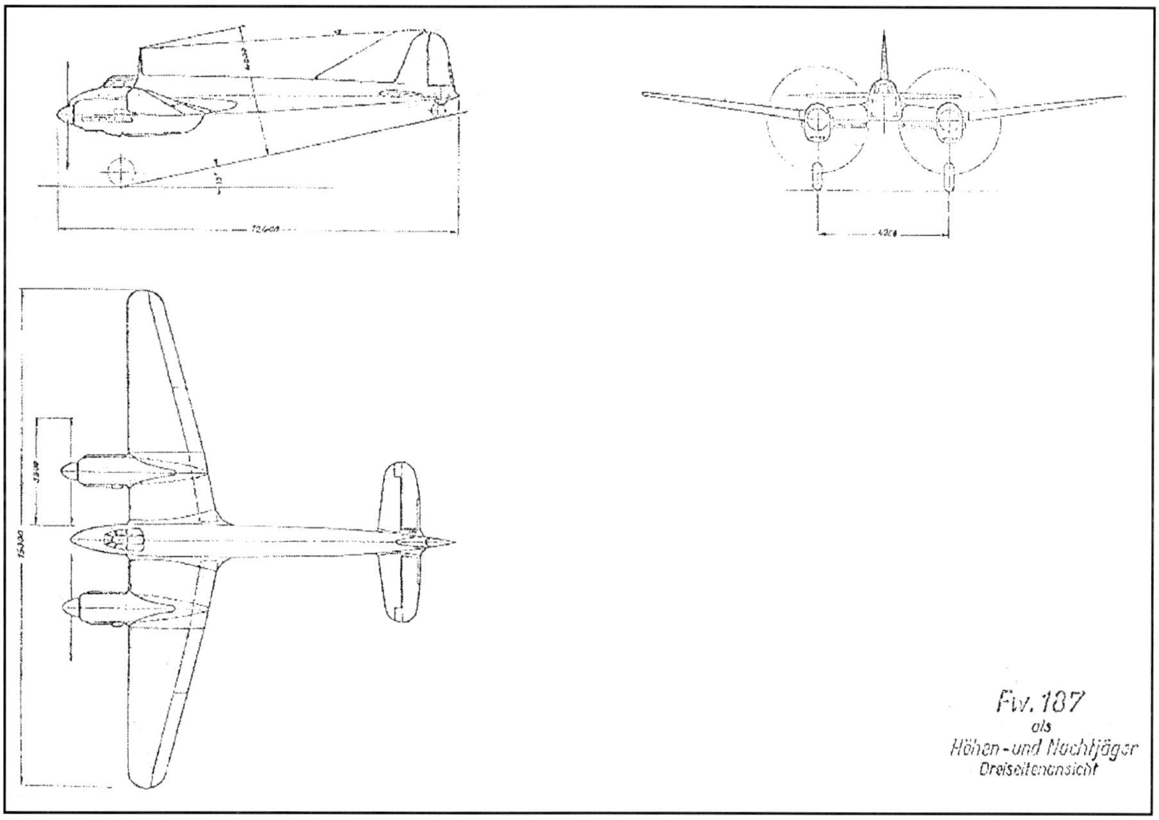

Three-view drawing of the Fw 187 high-altitude and night fighter.

The *Luftwaffe*'s first true high-altitude fighter was the Ta 152 H, a few examples of which entered service in the late days of the war.

In another, later type sheet concerning the single-seat high-altitude fighter, Focke Wulf listed performance figures for the Fw 187 H:

Gross weight	6050 kg
Wing area	30 m^2
Wing loading	202 kg/m^2
Armament	4 x MG 151
	2 x MG 151 and 4 x MG 131
	1 x MK 103 and 2 x MG 151 and 2 x MG 131
Power plant	2 x DB 605 engines from the Bf 109 G
	or 2 x DB 628
Performance	
with DB 605	max. speed = 725 km/h at 8100 m
	rate of climb = 21.2 m/s
	10000 m in 11 min.
	service ceiling 13300 m
with DB 628	max speed = 740 km/h at 10500 m
	rate of climb = 19.8 m/s
	10000 m in 10.6 min.
	service ceiling 13500 m

Although the high-altitude fighter version of the Fw 187 was given little consideration by the RLM, it is interesting to compare the performance of the Ta 152 with the calculated performance of the Fw 187 high-altitude fighter.

One should know that the *Luftwaffe* command was expecting Allied bombers to begin operating at higher altitudes in the near future. Both fighter producers, Focke Wulf and Messerschmitt, had received RLM contracts for the development of high-altitude fighters. Messerschmitt's high-altitude fighter was the Bf 109 H, while Focke Wulf began work on a high-altitude derivative of the Fw 190. When the Fw 187 was in development, Focke Wulf was already working on a version of the Fw 190 powered by a Daimler Benz DB 603 engine with a Heinkel Hirth exhaust-driven turbosupercharger. It was an obvious step, therefore, for the company to make a comparison of the performances of the Fw 187 and the Fw 190 high-altitude fighter.

In mid-1942 Focke Wulf ordered precise calculations for the Fw 190 alternatives to the Fw 187. In another performance sheet dated 22 June 1942, the rate of climb and combat performance of the Fw 187 H was compared to those of the Focke Wulf Fw 190 high-altitude fighter with a variety of engines. The Fw 187 with DB 605 engines (C3 fuel) was compared to the Fw 190 with the BMW 801 D (C3 fuel), DB 603 A (B4 fuel) and DB 603 H (C3

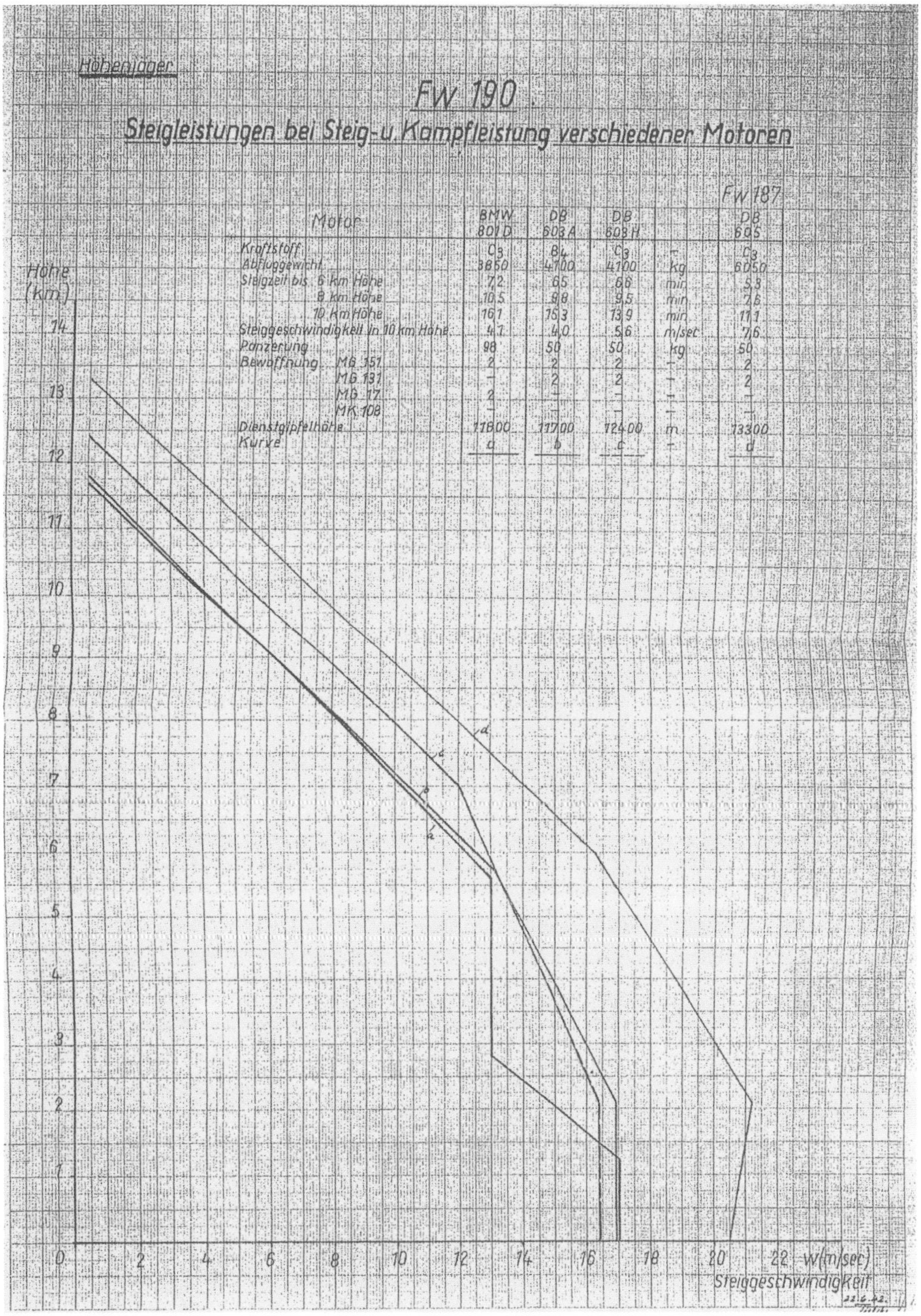

This graph depicting climb performance reveals the advantage possessed by the Fw 187 over the Fw 190.

fuel). As the accompanying diagram reveals, the various Fw 190 high-altitude fighter alternatives failed to surpass the Fw 187 H high-altitude fighter in any performance category (Curve D). The low-level climb rate of the Fw 187 was an exceptional 20 m/s. The Fw 187 was also the only aircraft capable of climbing above 13000 meters.

The Final End of the Fw 187

The Fw 187 V8 was to have been the prototype for the Fw 187 C-0 pre-production series. Focke Wulf records speak of a total of ten zero-series machines. Because of time constraints, and almost certainly pressure from the RLM, the C-1 production version was supposed to have been built in parallel with the pre-production series. This was not to happen, however.

The blow fell on 31 August 1942, in the midst of preparations for production. The RLM had decided on 11 July that a production contract was to be independent of the test result achieved with the prototypes, however one month later there was an abrupt about face. With the prototypes under construction, the responsible state secretary ordered Focke Wulf to immediately cease all work on the Fw 187. There is no direct proof of why the RLM took this decision, however there is indirect evidence. The following is from Focke Wulf correspondence: "Kaether[3] intends to wait for submission of the comparison between the He 219 and Fw 187 and delay the scrapping of components, as the technical Office may yet decide that the prototypes should be completed."

Focke Wulf had suffered the same fate as Messerschmitt. The aircraft was literally given the chop. The cancellation was not due to unfavorable test results, instead a decision once again had been made in favor of an aircraft which had not yet flown. Within just two months, a firm yes from the RLM had become an equally firm no. The RLM apparently did not know what it wanted. It abandoned its efforts to find a short-term replacement for the Me 210 and turned instead to a fundamental examination of the future requirements of the *Luftwaffe*. Unfortunately, it is impossible to determine why the RLM did not allow work on the two Fw 187 prototypes, which were at an advanced stage of construction, to continue until the type's actual performance could be determined. When development was halted, the two conversion aircraft, the Fw 187 V5/U1 and V7/U1, were in a disassembled state in the hangar in Adelheide. Two sets of engine mounts and accessories, but not the engines, had been delivered for installation. Internally, the company decided initially to set aside the parts from the damaged machine. After much argument as to what to do with the aircraft, in November 1942 a decision was made to scrap the disassembled prototypes. The same applied to the mock-up.

It was also decided that the two Danish machines earmarked for flight tests would not be returned to Focke Wulf, however it was too late to rescind the order. *Werknummer* 1968 arrived in Berlin from Vaerløse on 24 August 1942 and *Werknummer* 1974 from Warnemünde on the same day. In the midst of the confusion the undesired hand-over of the two aircraft was made. Soon afterwards, both Fw 187 A-0s sustained minor damage in an air raid on Bremen. In October 1942 it was decided to salvage parts needed for repairs from the two disassembled conversion machines. Repairs to the two Fw 187 A-0s was completed by 27 October 1942, however it was not until 8 February 1943 that GN+AG was flown back to Vaerløse by Oberleutnant Hans Müller. It is assumed that aircraft CA+WZ was also flown back to the aerial gunnery school. Focke Wulf's development effort is reflected in the figures. By the time work was halted, Focke Wulf had invested 26,640 engineer hours and 6,470 man-hours in the two prototypes. Focke Wulf calculated the cost to be 178,400 RM. These were wasted hours, which better control by the RLM could have directed toward other projects.

[3] Willy Kaether was Prof. Tank's assistant.

The Fw 187 Compared to Other German Types

The He 219 was selected over the Fw 187, at least for the night fighter role. Why was this? No official reason has yet been discovered. It is likely, however, that the events described here played a major role in the cancellation of the Fw 187.

Designation Purpose	**Fw 187 C-0** *Kampfzerstörer* Night fighter	**He 219 A-2** Fighter Night fighter	**Me 410 B-1** *Zerstörer* Fighter-bomber
Empty weight	5660 kg	9440 kg	7983 kg
Gross weight	8200 kg	12500 kg	11237 kg
Wingspan	15.3 m	18.5 m	16.4 m
Length	12.45 m	15.54 m	12.15 m
Height	3.35 m	4.1 m	3.7 m
Wing area	30 m^2	44.5 m^2	36.2 m^2
Wing loading	273.33 kg/m^2	280.89 kg/m^2	310 kg/m^2
Power plants	2 x DB 605A	2 x DB 603A	2 x DB 603G
Takeoff power	2 x 1475 PS	2 x 1750 PS	2 x 1740 PS
Fuel	B 4	B 4	B 4
Fuel capacity	1250 l	2600 l	2070 l
Range	1330 km	2150 km	1360 km
Range with auxiliary tanks	2100 km	2850 km	-
Takeoff distance	700 m	1050 m	960 m
Speed at low level	547 km/h	460 km/h[4)]	501 km/h
Maximum speed	682 km/h	560 km/h	630 km/h
at maximum boost altitude	7.1 km	6.4 kg	8.1 km
Landing speed	143 km/h	150 km/h	163 km/h
Landing distance	480 m	680m	NA
Rate of climb at low level	18 m/s[5)]	10 m/s	8.7 m/s
Time to climb to 2000 m	1.7 min	3.5 min	3.75 min
Time to climb to 4000 m	5.2 min	7.2 min	7.95 min
Time to climb to 8000 m	12.6 min	18 min	22.5 min
Service ceiling	10.5 km	8.9 km	9.5 km
Fuselage armament	4 x MG 151, 2 x MG 131, 1 x MG 181	4 x MG 151/20, 2 x MK 108	2 x MG 151, 2 x MG 17 2 x MG 131
Bomb load	max. 2000 kg	none	1000 kg

[4)] Performance figures without radar antennas and flame dampers.

[5)] Rate of climb at a gross weight of 6620 kg.
13.0 m/s rate of climb at gross weight of 8200 kg.

Though built in small numbers, the Heinkel He 219 night fighter was extremely successful. (Griehl)

The shortcomings displayed by the night fighter versions of the Bf 110 and Ju 88 became increasingly obvious when the RAF intensified its bombing campaign in 1942. Neither type had been designed for the night fighter role and by 1942 both were too slow to be effective. An effective night fighter was needed desperately. *General der Nachtjäger* Kammhuber was given special powers to search for a suitable aircraft. Following discussions with Kammhuber, in early September 1942 the RLM selected the He 219 as the best available candidate. It was also decided to develop the He 219 as a replacement for the Ju 88 C and Bf 110 G in the high-speed bomber role. This spelled the end for the Fw 187 night fighter. In spite of Focke Wulf's best efforts, the Fw 187 had no advocates in the RLM. According to chief test pilot Hans Sander, Kurt Tank never fully got over the cancellation of the Fw 187.

The Me 410, an improved version of the Me 210, took to the air at almost the exact time that the Fw 187 V5/U1 and V7/U1 were to have made their first flights. This development is described in the subsequent chapter. Was the performance of the Fw 187 C-0 inferior to that of the He 219 or Me 410, and was this the reason the aircraft was cancelled? For this reason alone it is interesting to compare the performance of the He 219 and Me 410 with that of the Fw 187, especially because of the controversy associated with the careers of the. The following comparisons are not intended to diminish the other two types.

In August 1942, when the decision between the Fw 187 and He 219 was being made, development of the He 219 was already at an advanced stage. Inspection of the He 219 mock-up had taken place in early 1942. Construction drawings were largely complete and the He 219 V1 was under construction. This was an extremely difficult situation for Focke Wulf. There had never been any preliminary discussions at the RLM level about also using the Fw 187 in the night fighter role. Heinkel undoubtedly had the development lead with the He 219. Originally conceived as a twin-engined bomber, the design was modified for the night fighter role. As a result, the first He 219 was able to take to the air on 15 November 1942. The first test mission was flown during the night of 11-12 June 1943. This proved extremely successful, with pilot *Oberst* Streib shooting down five British bombers. The He 219 was even capable of intercepting the fast de Havilland Mosquito. The He 219 was denied greater success by other factors. Official production contracts were minor, and only 268 aircraft were completed by the end of the war.

The first flight of the Fw 187 V5/U1 should have taken place at about the same time as the He 219. This alone would have been enough to demonstrate the Focke Wulf's impressive performance. Series production of the Fw 187 C could have begun in mid-1943. As the specifications reveal, the He 219 was much larger and heavier than the Fw 187, although this was partially compensated for by the former's more powerful DB 603 engines. The power plant question threatened the entire He 219 program. Like many other projects, the He 219 depended on an engine which was not yet available. Production aircraft were supposed to be powered by the 1,900-h.p. DB 603 G engine, however there were serious delays in development of this power plant. Heinkel turned to the 1,750-h.p. DB 603 A as an interim solution. As a result the He 219 was underpowered.

In comparing the performance of the Fw 187 and the He 219, it should be borne in mind that the radar antennas and flame dampers necessary for night fighter operations would have reduced the Fw 187's maximum speed by approximately 50 km/h. In spite of this, the Fw 187 would still have been a good 40 km/h faster than the He 219 at low level (500 km/h vs. 460 km/h) and 80 km/h faster at maximum boost altitude (640 km/h vs. 560 km/h). The Fw 187 thus had a slight performance advantage. Both types possessed excellent handling characteristics. As the Fw 187 was powered by the same engine as the Bf 109, installation of more powerful versions of the DB 605 would have been a simple matter. Even the bulkier BMW 801 D radial engine used by the Fw 190 could have been installed in the Fw 187 without difficulty.

The problem of unsatisfactory engines plagued the He 219 throughout its production life. The only true solution was offered by an engine which never reached the production stage, the Junkers Jumo 222. The lack of sufficiently powerful engines was a significant shortcoming. British test pilot Eric Brown wrote of the He 219: "The Heinkel was basically a good night fighter, however it "possessed a weakness which was one of the worst a twin-engined can have: it was underpowered." The Fw 187 did not have this shortcoming. In spite of this, it is acknowledged that the He 219 was an extremely successful night fighter.

Chief test pilot Hans Sander himself mentioned the Do 335 several times in connection with the Fw 187. Concerning the development of the Do 335, he remarked: "At that time Göring was opposed to a twin-engined, high-speed fighter and thus the Fw 187. he thought that two engines were too many for a fighter aircraft. As the Do 335 showed, these objections disappeared by the end of the war."

The Do 335 is regarded as the fastest German piston-engined fighter, therefore a comparison with the Fw 187 is appropriate. As information concerning the fighter version of the Fw 187 is limited, the comparison must be limited to the principal elements. A comparison with the Do 335 is also more difficult because development of the Dornier fighter took place much later. The Do 335 first flew on 26 October 1943, about one year after the scheduled maiden flight of the new Fw 187. The first pre-production aircraft were not delivered until late 1944. Part of the reason for the delay was the aircraft's tandem engine arrangement. This unusual configuration had to undergo extensive testing before it could be used in a high-performance fighter. The presence of a pusher engine made it necessary to develop and test an ejection seat to enable the pilot to safely exit the aircraft in an emergency. All these factors cost time. In comparing the two types, it should also be remembered that the Do 335, with its two DB 603 A engines, had available an additional 550 horsepower.

The Do 335 possessed a speed advantage of 12 km/h, and it required B4 fuel instead of the C3 fuel used by the Fw 187. There, too, the Fw 187 offered alternatives. Using the rule of thumb that an increase of 100 h.p. at the same weight results in an increase in speed of 10 km/h, installation of more powerful engines, such as the BMW 801, would have allowed the Fw 187 to make up this speed difference. Unfortunately, no performance figures for the new Fw 187 with BMW 801 D engines, which were in the same power class as the DB 603, have been found.

The DB 605-powered Fw 187 possessed a phenomenal rate of climb. It was capable of reaching 8000 meters in half the time required by the Do 335. This would have been a significant advantage in combat. It would be difficult to find another twin-engined fighter which could match this climbing performance. No prototype of the Fw 187 fighter version was ever built, and the type therefore never had the opportunity to demonstrate what it could do. But what of the Do 335?

In spite of Dornier's best efforts, the Do 335 was never delivered to a front-line unit. The aircraft's unconventional layout resulted in a lengthier development period. Only a few machines were completed by the end of the war. Production of the He 219 also suffered, and just 268 examples were built. We now know that pro-

The Do 335 was the *Luftwaffe*'s fastest piston-engined fighter. Shown here is the *Zerstörer* version armed with MK 103 cannon in the wings. (Dornier Archive)

duction of the He 219 was hindered by the bureaucracy of the RLM, even though it was the aircraft that the night fighter arm wanted. Pressure from the night fighter arm was the only reason why the fighter remained in production at all. In the end, neither the Do 335 nor the He 219 played any significant role in the air war. Both types had been selected in preference to the Fw 187, however, in the end other factors led to the demise of the Focke Wulf fighter.

Designation Purpose	**Focke Wulf Fw 187** high-altitude fighter	**Dornier Do 335 A-1** fighter-bomber
Empty weight	4905 kg	6350 kg
Gross weight	6050 kg	9510 kg
Wingspan	15.3 m	13.85 m
Length	12.45 m	13.8 m
Height	3.35 m	5 m
Wing area	30 m^2	38.5 m^2
Wing loading	202 kg/m^2	247 kg/m^2
Power plants	2 x DB 605A	2 x DB 603A
Takeoff power	2 x 1475 PS	2 x 1750 PS
Fuel	C 3	B 4
Maximum speed	725 km/h	732 km/h
at maximum boost altitude	8.1 km	7.1 km
Speed at low level	21.2 m/s	12.7 m/s
Time to climb to 6000 m	5.3 min	6 min
Time to climb to 8000 m	7.6 min	11.3 min
Time to climb to 10000 m	11.1 min	14.5 min
Service ceiling	13.3 km	11.3 km
Fuselage armament	2 MG 151, 2 MG 131	1 MK 103, 2 MG 151
Bomb load	-	500 kg

Messerschmitt Wins the *Zerstörer* Competition Again

While Focke Wulf was working hard to prepare the Fw 187 fighter version of production, the Messerschmitt company was redesigning the Me 210 for the *Zerstörer* role. To minimize the new heavy fighter's association with the ill-fated Me 210, Messerschmitt gave it a new designation, the Me 410. In March 1942 the Me 210 V17 demonstrated improve flight characteristics after receiving a lengthened fuselage. The first true prototype of the redesigned heavy fighter, the Me 410 V1, flew for the first time in the autumn of 1942. This approximated to the projected first flights of the converted Fw 187 V5/U1 and V7/U1. The Me 410 must therefore be viewed as a contemporary of the Fw 187.

Once again the power plant question proved a decisive factor. The RLM officials responsible for air armaments continually strove for standardization to minimize the number of power plants in production. Only in this way could the output of engines be maximized. For the Me 410 to be built in numbers the DB 603 had to be placed into large-scale production. At the beginning of 1942 the DB 603 had not been approved for large-scale production even for the Fw 190 fighter. It was feared that the additional production might come at the expense of the DB 605, which was needed for the Bf 109 fighter. The *Zerstörer* crisis facing the *Luftwaffe* in 1942 changed the situation, however. The DB 603 entered production. If the RLM had rejected the DB 603 it would have settled the fate of both the Me 410 and the He 219.

It can only be assumed that the favored *Zerstörer* version of the Fw 187 was cancelled for the same reasons. The RLM apparently did not want to accept any new risks with the new Fw 187. It had already waited too long for a replacement for the Bf 110. The redesigned and improved Me 410 proved to have acceptable flight characteristics, however it still could not match the outstanding performance and handling of the Fw 187. Production figures never reached the level required to have any effect on the military situation. When committed to operations in the Defense of the Reich, the Me 410 proved inferior to Allied escort fighters in terms of speed and maneuverability, resulting in heavy losses.

A performance comparison reveals that, in spite of its 1,750-h.p. engines, the Me 410 was clearly inferior to the Fw 187. The Focke Wulf fighter was 50 km/h faster at all altitudes and clearly superior in rate of climb. Both types had similar ranges with identical bomb loads. One feature of the Me 410 which stood out was its high wing loading of 310 kg/m°. When the Fw 187 first appeared it was criticized for its wing loading, however it appears that there was never any discussion of the Me 410's wing loading. The Me 410's performance must be seen as mediocre when compared to that of the Fw 187 and He 219. This must have been apparent to the RLM. Why it accepted the Me 410 without criticism remains a mystery.

Whether the *Zerstörer* version of the Fw 187 would have fared better than the Me 410 in the Defense of the Reich must remain pure speculation, however it was for just this purpose that Prof. Tank and his team designed the aircraft in 1937. It is interesting to note that in 1942 that the performance of the Fw 187 was once again equal to that of the *Luftwaffe*'s single-engined FTT, the Bf 109 and Fw 190. The Focke Wulf design was also equal or superior to the single-engined types in armament.

Not until the autumn of 1942 did an improved version of the Me 210, the Me 410, display an acceptable performance. Here are several Me 410 A-1s. (EADS Unternehmensarchiv Ottobrunn via Ebert)

The A-3 reconnaissance version of the Me 410. The Daimler Benz DB 603 was placed in large-scale production for the Me 410. (EADS Unternehmensarchiv Ottobrunn via Ebert)

Development of the Lockheed P-38 Lightning and de Havilland Mosquito

The redesigned Fw 187 never proceeded beyond the prototype construction stage. Although it never entered production, a surviving Specification makes it possible to form an impression of the machine's potential performance. A comparison between the redesigned Fw 187 and contemporary twin-engined designs produced by the Allied nations would therefore be extremely interesting. Would the Fw 187 C-0's performance have been equal to that of the Allied aircraft? The Lockheed P-38 Lighting and de Havilland Mosquito were both very successful twin-engined designs. Both were built in large numbers, with almost 10,000 P-38s and 7,781 Mosquitos being completed.

The Lockheed P-38 was designed as a high-altitude fighter aircraft. Development began in 1937 and the XP-38 flew for the first time on 27 January 1939. Among the P-38's unusual features were its twin boom layout and tricycle undercarriage. Production began in 1939-40, and the F-Series entered service in August 1942, during the period when the Fw 187 was being redesigned.

P-38 units flew their first bomber escort missions over Europe in October 1943. Equipped with two 625-liter drop tanks, the Lightnings were able to accompany the heavy bombers over Germany. This characteristic invites a direct comparison with the Fw 187. Both machines were very similar in weight, although the *Zerstörer* version of the Fw 187 carried a crew of two. Although the engines of both aircraft were similar in output, the P-38's were equipped with turbosuperchargers, which permitted a service ceiling of 13200 meters, significantly higher than that of the Fw 187. The Fw 187

The Lockheed P-38 Lightning.

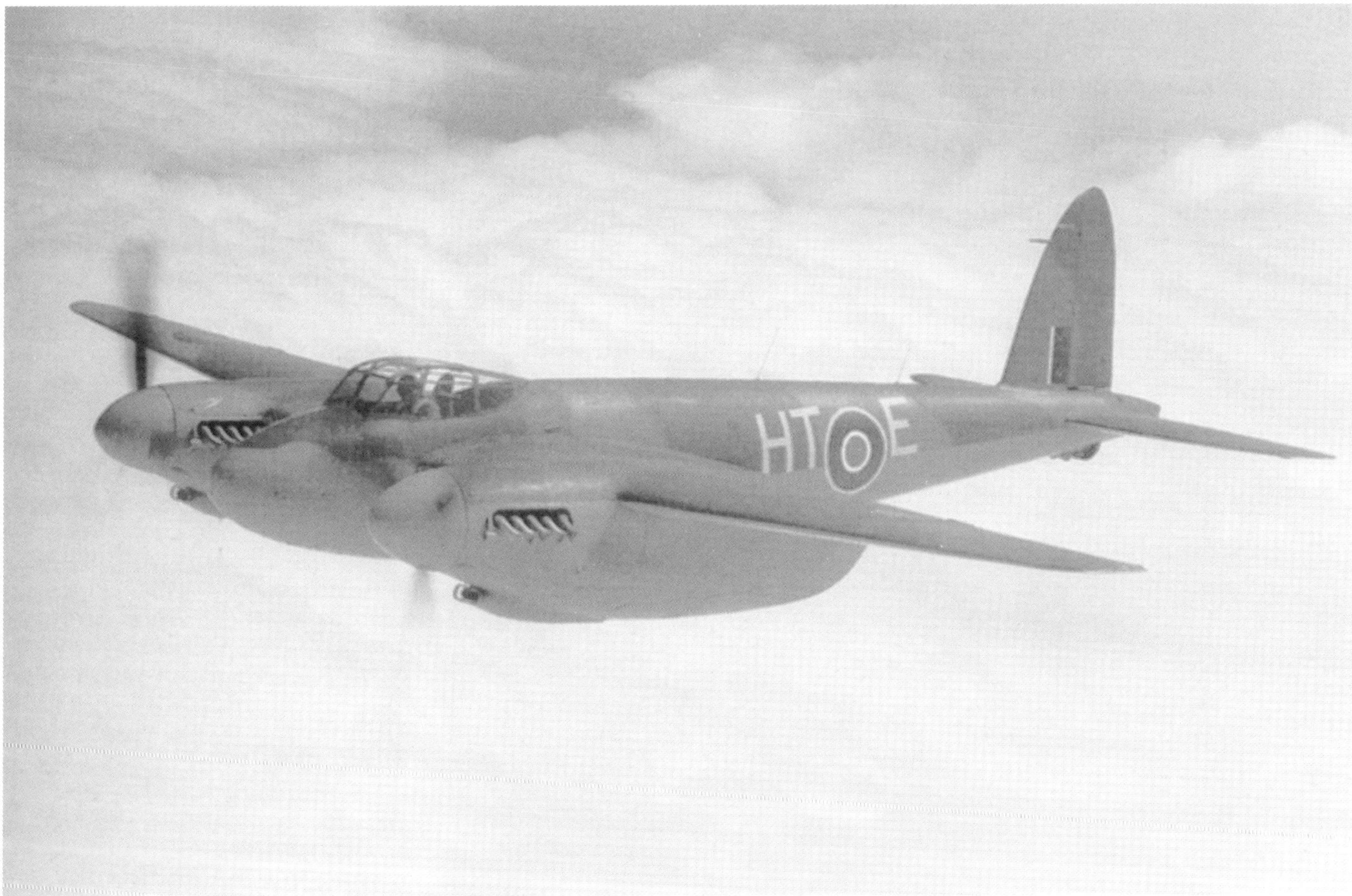

The de Havilland Mosquito was the standard against which German night fighters were measured. In spite of a massive effort, the German aviation industry failed to produce a piston-engined night fighter which could match the performance of the Mosquito.

Zerstörer lacked a pressurized cockpit, which would have been necessary for operations at such altitudes. The proposed high-altitude fighter version of the Fw 187 would have been more competitive in this regard. Another area in which the Lightning had the edge was range. With a fuel capacity of 1250 liters, the P-38 had a range of 3640 km. Even with two 900-liter drop tanks, the Fw 187's range was just 2100 km.

The P-38 was also heavily armed. One 20-mm cannon and four 12.7-mm machine-guns were grouped in the nose, which was reminiscent of that of the Bf 110. In terms of armament the Fw 187 was equal to the P-38.

Unlike the Lockheed P-38 and Focke Wulf Fw 187, the de Havilland Mosquito was designed to be made of wood. Development work began in 1938 and the Mosquito was designed as a high-speed bomber powered by two Rolls Royce Merlin engines. Because of the aircraft's high speed, no defensive armament was carried. Begun as a private project, the Mosquito soon attracted the attention of the Air Ministry, which ordered fifty aircraft. The first Mosquito took to the air on 25 November 1940. Less than a year later, in September 1941, Mosquitos flew the first photo reconnaissance missions over occupied Europe and Germany. This was one of the Mosquito's most important operational roles. Carrying additional fuel tanks in the bomb bay, the Mosquito was capable of penetrating deep into German airspace. These unarmed reconnaissance machines were so fast that no German fighter was capable of catching them. This was part of the reason for the Mosquito's legendary reputation.

The Mosquito proved capable of almost every operational role. The first units to equip with the bomber version were formed in early 1942. Like the reconnaissance variant, the Mosquito bomber's speed allowed it to avoid interception.

A high-altitude fighter version of the Mosquito powered by two-stage Merlin engines was developed in response to sorties over the United Kingdom by high-flying Ju 86 P reconnaissance-bombers. Designated the Mosquito NF Mk. XV, the high-altitude fighter was abandoned in favor of high-altitude Spitfires. The Mosquito proved so successful that production was expanded to Canada and Australia.

The first night fighter version of the Mosquito entered service in 1942. The NF Mk. II was followed by improved versions. The Mosquito night fighter's success is reflected in its tally of approximately 600 German aircraft destroyed by the end of the war.

Another vital role for the Mosquito was that of pathfinder. Flying ahead of the bomber stream, Mosquitos marked targets for the heavy bombers. Equipped with special bombing aids, the Mosquito was capable of bombing through cloud. Later in the war de Havilland produced a high-altitude bomber version of the Mosquito equipped with a pressurized cockpit. The Mosquito Mk. B XVI was capable of reaching 665 km/h and appeared over Germany in late 1944.

The success of this wooden aircraft resulted in demands for the German aviation industry to produce a similar design. Focke Wulf responded with the Ta 154, however the design was not a success and only a few examples of the German *Moskito* were built.

Comparison of the Redesigned Fw 187, Lockheed P-38 Lightning and de Havilland Mosquito

Obviously this comparison must be a theoretical exercise. The Fw 187 C would have entered production in 1943. For the purpose of this comparison, versions of the Lightning and Mosquito have been selected which entered service at approximately the same time.

Designation	Fw 187 C-0 Falke	P-38 L Lightning	Mosquito FB VI
Purpose	*Kampfzerstörer*	Fighter aircraft	Fighter-bomber Empty weight
Gross weight	5660 kg	5800 kg	6486 kg
Wingspan	8200 kg	9960 kg	8845 kg
Length	15.3 m	15.85 m	16.51 m
Height	3.35 m	2.98 m	4.66 m
Wing area	30 m²	30.47 m²	42.18 m²
Wing loading	273.33 kg/m²	255.6 kg/m²	230.48 kg/m²
Power plants	2 x DB 605A	2 x Allison V-1710-111	2 x RR Merlin 25
Takeoff power	2 x 1475 PS	2 x 1475 PS	2 x 1475 PS
Fuel	B 4	100/130 Octane	100/130 Octane
Fuel capacity	1250 l	1575 l + 1278 l[7]	2060 l
Range	1330 km	1947 km	1962 km
Range with auxiliary tanks	2100 km	2870 km	2132 km[8]
Takeoff distance	480 m	730 m	-
Speed at low level	547 km/h	563 km/h	541 km/h
Maximum speed	682 km/h	667 km/h	612 km/h
at maximum boost altitude	7.1 km	7.62 km	3.96 km
Landing speed	143 km/h	155 km/h	-
Rate of climb at low level	18 m/s[6]	18.6 m/s	12.7 m/s
Service ceiling	10.5 km	13.2 km	10.4 km
Fuselage armament	4 MG 151, 2 MG 131	1 x 20 mm Hispano MK	4 x 20 mm Hispano MK
	1 MG 81	4 x 12.7 mm Browning	4 x 7.69 mm Browning MG
Bomb load	max. 2000 kg	2 x 725 kg	max. 907 kg (2000 lb)

Conclusion: An examination of the performance figures above reveal that the Fw 187 C-0 was at least the equal of the two Allied machines. The information in the table speaks for itself. On paper at least, the *Zerstörer* version of the Fw 187 had certain advantages over the fighter-bomber version of the Mosquito.

[6] Rate of climb at a gross weight of 6620 kg. Rate of climb 13 m/s at a gross weight of 8200 kg.

[7] With two 165 U.S. gallon combat tanks.

[8] With 100-gallon auxiliary tanks.

New Projects

The first of the so-called 1,000 bomber raids struck Cologne on the night of 30 May 1942. These attacks were on a scale which far surpassed anything seen before. Explosions and fires inflicted massive damage and inflicted heavy civilian casualties. Essen, Bremen and other cities were attacked in rapid succession. The success of these operations was closely linked to the use by the RAF of pathfinder aircraft to mark targets. The high-speed Mosquito bombers used in this role were immune to interception by German night fighters. The principal German night fighter aircraft were versions of the Ju 88 and Bf 110, heavy machines whose maximum speed

The twin-engined Focke Wulf Ta 154 was supposed to be Germany's answer to the de Havilland Mosquito. Production was halted abruptly and only a few aircraft reached the *Luftwaffe*. (Focke Wulf)

In this photograph the Focke Wulf Fw 187 Falke displays its clean lines. The sleek design undoubtedly deserved its name.

was reduced by drag-producing radar antennas. The German command was aware of these shortcomings and immediately called for an aircraft which was capable of intercepting the speedy Mosquitos. Although the Fw 187 possessed the performance necessary to counter the Mosquito, it was not selected. Shortages of strategic materials and the success of the wood construction used in the Mosquito led the RLM to call for a similar wooden fighter. The task of developing the new machine was given to Focke Wulf. The Focke Wulf designers came up with an entirely new design, which within the company was designated the Ta 211. The new aircraft was to be of mixed construction. The officials in charge of development and procurement must have known that it would be at least two years before the new aircraft could enter service, two years in which the Mosquitos could roam the skies over Germany unhindered. Instead of adopting the Fw 187, whose design was complete, they proceeded with the new twin-engined aircraft, the Focke Wulf Ta 154 *Moskito*.

The Do 335 is considered to represent the apex of German piston-engine fighter design. Considering the impressive performance expected from the improved Fw 187 C, it is possible that it could have made the Do 335 fighter-*Zerstörer* completely redundant, as it would have been available much sooner. Unlike some of its contemporaries, the Fw 187 had not exhausted its development potential and the aircraft could have taken advantage of more powerful versions of the DB 605 to further improve its performance. The installation of power plants in the 2,000-h.p. range would have made possible maximum speeds on the order of 750 km/h.

Messerschmitt did not completely solve the *Luftwaffe*'s *Zerstörer* dilemma. The air war took a different direction, and the Messerschmitt aircraft had to serve in the Defense of the Reich, a role for which they were not designed. The inability of the *Luftwaffe*'s twin-engined fighters to match the performance of the enemy's escort fighters ultimately resorted in the *Zerstörer* pilots being forced to convert to single-seat fighters. This abrupt change also resulted in casualties among the former *Zerstörer* pilots. Had the Fw 187 entered service, this probably would not have happened. Moreover, the presence of a capable twin-engined heavy fighter would have allowed the *Luftwaffe*'s Bf 109s and Fw 190s to return

This photograph illustrates the striking similarities in general configuration shared by the Mosquito and the Fw 187.

to their true fighter role. Had the Fw 187's performance lived up to expectations, it would have been at least equal to the enemy's escort fighters.

The last known operational sortie by a Fw 187 took place on 29 August 1943, when the Danish Army was disarmed. The following entry appears in the diary of the CIC Denmark: "0630 hours. Air Commander Copenhagen reports 1 Bf 109, 2 Ju 88, 1 Ju 87, 1 Bf 110 and 1 Fw 187 scrambled over Copenhagen." Of the two remaining Fw 187 A-0s, one is known to have continued flying with the Vaerløse Aerial Gunnery School until May 1944.

The Fw 187 A-0 as a Flying Model

The Focke Wulf Fw 187 remains a source of fascination to this day, especially among modelers. One modeler, Dipl.Ing. Ernst Heinrich Neumann, has created a flying scale model (1 : 5.2) of the Fw 187 A-0 in the markings of the Vaerløse Aerial Gunnery School. Photographs of the model on the ground and in the air have a very realistic appearance. According to Herr Neumann, the Fw 187 model has excellent flight characteristics.

A 1 : 5.2 scale flying model of the Fw 187. The model is powered by two 2.5-h.p. chainsaw engines and weighs 18.5 kg. Wingspan is 2.94 meters, length 2.13 meters. (Neumann)

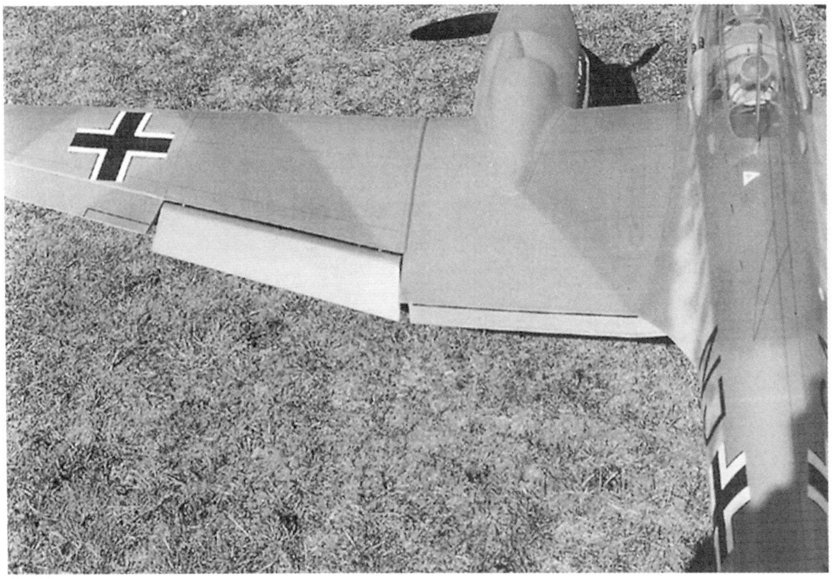

These photographs reveal the level of detail incorporated into the model.

These photographs of the Fw 187 model in flight are very impressive. Overall NJ+CA makes a very realistic impression. (Neumann)

Prototypes of the Fw 187

Aircraft	Code	Werk-Nr.	Purpose	Power Plants	First Flight	Remarks
Fw 187 V1	D-AXAK	949	Heavy fighter, single-seater	Jumo 210 D	10/04/37	First flight by Kurt Tank, scheduled tests at Rechlin. Crashed at Bremen on 14/05/38, 100% write-off, pilot Paul Bauer killed.
Fw 187 V2	D-AZAX D-AANA	950	Heavy fighter, single-seater	Jumo 210 D	14/06/37	First flight by Kurt Tank, test flown at Rechlin. Undercarriage failure at Rechlin, minor damage, delivered to RLM on 2/8/39.
Fw 187 V3	D-AODE	1707	Heavy fighter, Single-seater	Jumo 210 G	7/38	First flight (planned summer 1937) seriously delayed. Larger radiators, ejector exhausts and Jumo 210 G engines. In Rechlin Oct. 1938 for weapons trials. Delivered to the RLM on 2/8/39, back in Rechlin on 21/9/39. Crashed as a result of engine fire.
Fw 187 V4	D-ORHP	1966	Heavy fighter, two-seater	Jumo 210 G	27/10/38	RLM contract 10 07 038, first flight by Kurt Mehlhorn. Focke Wulf testing from 27/10/38 to 6/2/39. Transferred to the RLM on 23/9/39, scrapped.
Fw 187 V5	CI+NY	1976	Hot-cooling experiments	DB 601 V	October 1939	RLM contract 10 07 061. Test bed for hot-cooling. Delivered to RLM on 8/4/40. Parked 7/41. Focke Wulf trials concluded 2/42.

Fw 187 V5/U1	CI+NY	1976	Test bed for Fw 187 C *Zerstörer*	DB 605 A	planned Oct. 42	RLM contract 50 07 012 for conversion of first prototype for the Fw 187 C-0. Conversion begun, not completed, scrapped 12/42.
Fw 187 V6	GN+AG	1974	Weapons test-bed	Jumo 210 G		Test bed for new weapons installation of 4 MG 17 + 2 MG FF. Also used to test new windscreen for A-0 series.
Fw 187 V7	—	1977	Prototype Fw 187 B-0	DB 601 E planned	planned 10/39	RLM contract 10 07 062. Aircraft nitially earmarked for record attempt with DB 601 engines. Only 80% completed, then modified back to Fw 187 B-0, test bed for evaporation cooling. Delivered to RLM on 12/4/40, Focke Wulf trials completed 2/42.
Fw 187 V7/U1	—	1977	Prototype Fw 187 C *Zerstörer*	DB 605 A	planned Nov. 42	RLM contract 50 07 013 for conversion to second Fw 187 C-0 prototype. Conversion begun, not completed. Scrapped in December 1942.
Fw 187 V8	—	0001	Fw 187 C-0 *Zerstörer*	DB 605 A	spring 1943	First pre-production machine, not completed.
Fw 187_{Br}		—	Static test airframe for Fw 187 C			Not completed

Fw 187 Pre-production Aircraft

Type	Code	Werk-Nr.	Purpose	Power Plants	First Flight	Remarks
Fw 187 A-0	D-OSNP (?)	1967	Heavy fighter Fw 187 S1	Jumo 210 G	*Sept 39*	Contract 10 07 039, delivered to the RLM disassembled on 23/9/39, subsequently scrapped.
Fw 187 A-0	D-OVRB CA+WZ Yellow 4	1968	Heavy fighter Fw 187 S2	Jumo 210 G	*June 39*	Contract 10 07 039. Undercarriage tests at Argus/Berlin in July 1939. In Vaerløse until July 1942, converted there to MK 101. Returned to Berlin for testing associated with the Fw 187 C, later transferred back to Vaerløse.
Fw 187 A-0	D-OTGN NJ+CA Yellow 5 (?)	1969	Heavy fighter Fw 187 S3	Jumo 210 G	*May 39*	Contract 10 07 040. To Rheinmetall-Borsig in Fassberg for trials on 23/10/1939. Returned to Bremen on 8/5/40, Industry Defense, then Vaerløse. April 1941 stalled on approach to land, came down in forest. Aircraft destroyed, pilot seriously injured. Accident in Vaerløse (?).
		1970-1973				Not Fw 187 *Werknummer*, these serial numbers were assigned to the Fw 58 V5, Fw 186 V1 and Fw 186 V2. *Werknummer* 1973 not assigned.

Fw 187 A-0	D-OPBQ GN+AG Yellow 1	1974	Heavy fighter Fw 187 S4	Jumo 210 G	*May 39*	Contract 10 07 40. Tested at Rechlin 1939, aircraft in Vaerløse until July 1942. Returned to Bremen for flight trials associated with the Fw 187 C. Transferred back to Vaerløse on 8/2/43, probably flew there until May 1944.
Fw 187 A-0	D-???? CI+NX Yellow 7	1975	Heavy fighter Fw 187 S5	Jumo 210 G	*Sept. 39*	Contract 10 07 40. Landing accident caused by undercarriage failure at Hoya on 2/7/40, aircraft subsequently scrapped.
Fw 187 B-0	—	1977	Heavy fighter	DB 601 E	*Oct. 39*	Intended for record attempt as Fw 187 V7 powered by DB 601 engines (see Fw 187 V7).
Fw 187 B-0	—	1978	Heavy fighter	DB 601	7/11/1939[9]	RLM contract 10 07 063, aircraft 60% completed.
Fw 187 B-0	—	1979	Heavy fighter	DB 601	10/10/1939[9]	RLM contract 10 07 063, aircraft 60% completed, not scrapped.

Note: The civil registrations of the five Fw 187 A-0s are known, however with three exceptions these cannot be assigned to specific *Werknummer* with certainty. Those that are known are D-OTGN for WNr. 1969, D-OVRB for WNr. 1968 and D-OPBQ for WNr. 1974. Other registrations were D-OSNP, D-ORVH and D-ODXG.

The existence of an aircraft "Yellow 5" in the Industry Defense *Staffel* has yet be confirmed.

Dates in italics are delivery dates to the RLM.

[9] Delivery of components to the supervisor of construction.

Mitteilung an Herrn Gaube.

Nachfolgend geben wir Ihnen die gewünschten Flüge auf, die Herr Direktor Tank auf dem Flugzeugmuster Fw 187 in der Zeit vom 10.4.37 bis 9.7.40 durchgeführt hat:

1.	10.4.37	Bremen	Werkstattflug		$16^{44} - 16^{58}$	14 Min.
2.	25.4.37	"	"		$10^{52} - 11^{03}$	11 "
3.	22.5.37	"	Probeflug	D-AXAK	$9^{05} - 9^{42}$	37 "
4.	14.6.37	"	Werkstattflug		$15^{55} - 16^{17}$	22 "
5.	7.7.37	"	Probeflug	D-AZAX	$7^{24} - 7^{42}$	18 "
6.	17.7.37	"	Werkstattflug	"	$10^{45} - 10^{52}$	7 "
7.	"	"	"	"	$11^{24} - 11^{42}$	18 "
8.	30.9.37	"	"	D-AANA	$16^{00} - 16^{45}$	45 "
9.	28.10.37	"	"	"	$10^{48} - 11^{03}$	15 "
10.	19.7.38	"	Probeflug		$15^{16} - 15^{37}$	21 "
11.	28.8.38	"	Werkstattflug		$12^{12} - 12^{36}$	24 "
12.	3.9.38	"	"	D-AODE	$10^{01} - 10^{20}$	19 "
13.	4.9.38	"	"	"	$9^{37} - 9^{41}$	4 "
14.	"	"	"	"	$9^{42} - 9^{52}$	10 "
15.	"	"	"	"	$9^{54} - 10^{15}$	21 "
16.	16.9.38	"	"	"	$12^{10} - 12^{25}$	15 "
17.	24.9.38	"	Vorführung	"	$11^{22} - 12^{10}$	48 "
18.	26.9.38	"	Werkstattflug	"	$16^{29} - 16^{39}$	10 "
19.	14.11.38	"	Probeflug	D-ODXG	$16^{23} - 16^{37}$	14 "
20.	22.11.38	"	"	"	$12^{27} - 12^{47}$	20 "
21.	28.2.39	"	"	D-OTGN	$10^{47} - 11^{04}$	17 "
22.	9.3.39	"	"	D-ORVH	$8^{21} - 8^{43}$	23 "
23.	"	"	"	D-OVRB	$16^{10} - 16^{20}$	10 "
24.	8.11.39	"	Werkstattflug		$10^{27} - 11^{13}$	46 "
25.	"	"	Platzflug	CI+NX	$11^{20} - 11^{30}$	10 "
26.	10.1.40	"	"	"	$11^{06} - 11^{21}$	15 "
27.	11.1.40	"	Werkstattflug	"	$11^{33} - 11^{50}$	17 "
28.	30.4.40	Bremen-Jever			$8^{33} - 8^{47}$	10 "
29.	2.5.40	Marx-Bremen			$18^{47} - 19^{10}$	23 "
30.	5.5.40		Werkflug	7	$10^{27} - 11^{13}$	46 "
31.	"	Bremen-Marx		7	$15^{15} - 15^{35}$	20 "
32.	"	Marx-Bremen		7	$17^{52} - 18^{15}$	23 "

- 2 -

33.	12.5.40	Bremen	Überwachungsflug	7	5^{43} - 6^{34}	51 Min.
34.	13.5.40	"	Werkstattflug	7	5^{44} - 6^{35}	51 "
35.	"	"	Sperrflug	7	8^{02} - 9^{13}	71 "
36.	15.5.40	"	Flakerkennungs- u. Übungsflug		8^{02} - 9^{12}	70 "
37.	23.5.40	"	" "	7	7^{33} - 9^{25}	52 "
38.	27.5.40	"	" "	7	7^{20} - 8^{05}	45 "
39.	28.5.40	Bremen-Jever			14^{32} - 14^{52}	20 "
40.	"	Jever-Bremen			17^{49} - 18^{09}	20 "
41.	29.5.40	Bremen-Jever			15^{59} - 16^{20}	21 "
42.	2.6.40	Jever-Bremen			19^{58} - 20^{23}	25 "
43.	6.6.40	Jever-Bremen			15^{45} - 16^{07}	22 "
44.	16.6.40	Bremen	Überwachungsflug		6^{24} - 7^{44}	80 "
45.	21.6.40	"	Einsatzflug	CI+NX	10^{16} - 11^{20}	4 "
46.	24.6.40	"	"	7	19^{00} - 19^{26}	26 "
47.	9.7.40	"	"	1	11^{05} - 12^{08}	63

Bremen, den 21. Januar 1942
TV/Ge./Peu./2

A list of all flights by Kurt Tank in the Fw 187 up to 9 July 1940.

Bibliography

Focke Wulf Documents
Minutes of Meetings:

No. 211 Fw 187 windscreen, dated 14/1/1936
No. 212 Fw 187 second mock-up inspection, dated 28/1/1936
No. 228 Discussion of power plants to be considered for the Fw 187 V1, V2 and V3, dated 7/5/1936
No. 324 Discussion of inspection of Fw 187 V2 equipment, dated 9/7/1937
No. 372 Fw 187 mock-up inspection, further developments, dated 21/12/1937
373-189-9 Protected fuel tanks in Fw 187 0-Series, dated 5/1/1938
11-11-11 Fw 187 V4 and A-0 power plants, dated 21/01/1938
12-12-12 Fw 187 electrical equipment (further development), dated 26/1/1938
393-187-13 Fw 187 working discussion, flexibly-mounted guns, dated 22/2/1938
15-15-15 Fw 187 V4 mock-up inspection, dated 7/4/1938
441-187-17 Discussion of Fw 187 V4 and V5 power plants, dated 17/8/1938
476-187-20 Discussion of evaporation cooling for Fw 187 V5, dated 20/10/1938
Memorandum on strength and design of the Fw 187 V4 fuselage, dated 9/12/1938

Fw 187 Specifications:

Specification No. 181 "Fw 187 V4 Heavy Fighter"- June 1938
Specification No. 233 "Twin-Engined Stuka (Single-Seat)"- July 1940
Specification No. 235 "Twin-Engined Stuka (Two-Seat)"- August 1940
Specification No. 250 "Twin-Engined *Kampfzerstörer*" – August 1942
Fw 187 High-Altitude Fighter Investigation of June 1942

Cost Summaries:

Cost Summary Contract 10 07 038 for the Fw 187 V4, *Werknummer* 1966, dated 19/1/1940
Cost Summary Contract 10 07 039 for two Fw 187 A-0, *Werknummer* 1967 and 1968
Cost Summary Contract 10 07 040 for three Fw 187 A-0, *Werknummer* 1969, 1974 and 1975 dated 22/1/1940
Cost Summary Contract 10 07 061 for the Fw 187 V5, *Werknummer* 1976, dated 23/8/1940
Cost Summary Contract 10 07 062 for Fw 187 B-0, *Werknummer* 1977, dated 25/8/1940
Cost Summary Contract 10 07 063 for two Fw 187 V5 aircraft, *Werknummer* 1978 and 1979

Fw 187 New

Weekly Reports Fw 187 No. 1 of 1/6/1942 to No. 4 of 7/9/1942 (Juckstock Group)
Focke Wulf Development Bulletin dated 19/8/1942
Fw 187 Bulletins of 1/9/1942, 7/9/1942, 22/9/1942, 30/09/1942
Fw 187 Bulletin Concerning *Werknummer* 1968 and 1974 of 15/10/1942
Memorandum Equipping Fw 187 with MK 101, dated 18/9/1942
Cost summary for redesign of Fw 187, dated 22/09/1942
Conversion of Fw 187 *Werknummer* 1976 and 1977, dated 26/10/42, 12/11/42, 19/11/42 and 2/12/42

List of Contracts Fw 187 New

10 07 080 Redesign and readying for production of Fw 187 C-0 construction drawings, 25/7/1942
10 07 081 Handling quality tests of both Fw 187s from Denmark, 25/7/1942
10 07 082 Construction of a Fw 187_{Br} static test airframe (for DB 605)
10 07 083 Redesign and conversion plus construction of additional jigs for the conversion of Fw 187 with DB 605 engines, 25/7/1942
10 07 084 Design and construction of a fuselage mock-up for Fw 187 with DB 605 engines, 28/7/1942
10 07 085 Change to materials other than light metals and completion of associated tests for the Fw 187 with DB 605 engines, 15/8/1942
50 07 012 Conversion of Fw 187 aircraft Werk-Nr. 1976 with DB 605 engines, 4/7/1942
50 07 013 Conversion of Fw 187 Werk-Nr. 1977 (2nd conversion aircraft) to DB 605 engines, 21/7/1942

Flight Reports

Fw 187 flight notes by Director Tank from 10/04/1937 to 9/07/1940
Type testing and performance figures for the Fw 187 V2 in Rechlin, 24/6/1938
Rechlin flight notes for the Fw 187 V2 and Fw 187 V3
Flight reports *Werknummer* 1968 dated 16/3/40, 20/3/40, 27/3/40, 2/4/40, 4/4/40, 6/4/40 and 8/4/40
Flight reports *Werknummer* 1974 dated 16/3/40, 20/3/40, 27/3/40 and 8/4/40
Flight reports *Werknummer* 1975 dated 2/4/40, 3/4/40 and 4/4/40

Other Documents Related to the Fw 187

List of Fw 187 Prototypes by the RLM LC II / 1 b
E-Stelle Rechlin – Radio Equipment of the Fw 187 V4 and 0-Series, 7/11/1938
Fw 187 V5 evaporator development, 19/10/38
Memorandum on evaporation cooling and the Fw 187 V5 – Visit to Focke Wulf by Daimler Benz staff from 13/9 to 23/9/1939
Rigidity measurements of trim tabs of 1968, 1969 and 1974, Oct.-Nov. 1939
RLM memo on cost summary of Fw 187 V1-V3, 29/3/1940
Comparison of design hours for various Focke Wulf designs, 24/7/1941
DVL accident report

Daimler Benz Documents

DB memorandum on evaporation cooling, 30/12/1938
Test Report 10 18 101 192 Evaporation Cooling, 24/4/39
1st Test Report 10 18 101 425 Focke Wulf evaporation cooling, 19/5/39
2nd Test Report 10 18 101 425 Focke Wulf evaporation cooling, 25/5/39
Test Report 10 18 101 544 Fw 187 V5 Intake Scoop, 1/8/1939
DB 605 A-B performance sheet, 4/43
DB 601 H performance sheet

Specification Sheets

Messerschmitt Bf 110 G-3 Aircraft Data, 9/8/1943
Messerschmitt Performance Sheet Me 210 A-1
Messerschmitt Data Sheet Me 410 B-1, 13/4/1943
RLM GL/A-Rü IA Identification features Bf 110 G-2/Me 210 C-2, 1/6/1942

Books/Magazines

Conradis, Heinz: *Nerven, Herz und Rechenschieber:* Kurt Tank – Flieger, Forscher, Konstrukteur

Heumann, Gert: *Focke Wulf Fw 187 Falke*

Heumann, Gert: *Falken und Mosquitoes, Flugwelt 1957/2*

Kosin, Rüdiger: *Die Entwicklung der deutschen Jagdflugzeuge*

Munson, Kenneth: *Die Weltkrieg II Flugzeuge*

Redemann, Hans: *Die bahnbrechenden Konstruktionen im* Flugzeugbau

Redemann, Hans: *Die Falke aus Bremen, Flugrevue 5/89*

Robertson, Bruce: *Westland Whirlwind*

Schmoll, Peter: *Luftangriff, Regensburg und die Messerschmitt-* Werke im Fadenkreuz 1939-1945

Wagner, Wolfgang: *Kurt Tank – Konstrukteur und Testpilot*

Luftwissen 1940, Vol. 7 *Ein neuer Zerstörer Focke Wulf Fw 187*

To the following I wish to express my sincere appreciation for their help and support: Peter Achs, Fritz Carstens, Frank Berger, Sven Carlsen, Rick Chapman, Eddy Creek, Hans Joachim Ebert, Oberst a.D Wilhelm Göbel von der Gemeinschaft der Jagdflieger, Manfred Griehl, Jörgen Helme, Dieter Herwig, Herbert Kruse, Michael Meyer, Ernst-Heinrich Neumann, Peter Petrick, Stephen Ransom, Christoph Regel, Roland Remp, Heinz Rode, Günter Sengfelder, Gerhard Stemmer, Marton Szigeti, Udo Trümper, Eberhard Weber, Herrn Heintzer und Dr. Niebaum der DaimlerChrysler AG, dem EADS Unternehmensarchiv Bremen und Ottobrunn und insbesondere Cheftestpilot Hans Sander (V). Special thanks go to Peter Petrick, who made available his archive of Fw 187 photographs. Unless otherwise noted, all photographs are from the Petrick and Hermann Archives.